TRUE BLUE *Quilts*

Sew 15 Reproduction Quilts Honoring 19th-Century Designs

ANNETTE PLOG

KANSAS CITY STAR QUILTS
an imprint of C&T Publishing

PUBLISHER: Amy Marson

CREATIVE DIRECTOR: Gailen Runge

EDITORS: Karla Menaugh and Liz Aneloski

TECHNICAL EDITOR: Debbie Rodgers

COVER DESIGNER: Page + Pixel

BOOK DESIGNER: April Mostek

PRODUCTION COORDINATOR: Tim Manibusan

PRODUCTION EDITORS: Jennifer Warren and Nicole Rolandelli

ILLUSTRATOR: Valyrie Gillum

PHOTO ASSISTANTS: Carly Jean Marin and Mai Yong Vang

STYLE PHOTOGRAPHY by Lucy Glover and
INSTRUCTIONAL PHOTOGRAPHY by Diane Pedersen
of C&T Publishing Inc., unless otherwise noted

Published by Kansas City Star Quilts, an imprint of
C&T Publishing, Inc., P.O. Box 1456, Lafayette, CA 94549

Library of Congress Cataloging-in-Publication Data

Names: Plog, Annette, 1955- author.

Title: True blue quilts : sew 15 reproduction quilts honoring
19th-century designs / Annette Plog.

Description: Lafayette, CA : Kansas City Star Quilts, 2017.

Identifiers: LCCN 2016034410 | ISBN 9781617453403 (soft cover)

Subjects: LCSH: Patchwork--United States--Patterns. | Quilting--United States--Patterns.

Classification: LCC TT835 .P616 2017 | DDC 746.46/041--dc23

LC record available at https://lccn.loc.gov/2016034410

Printed in the USA

10 9 8 7 6 5 4 3 2

Dedication

To my supportive and understanding husband, Jim; my children, Lauren and David, and their respective spouses, Clay and Alyson; and my grandchildren, Lucy, Joshua, and Riley—the loves of my life. All of you encourage and inspire me every day to smile and laugh and enjoy the journey.

To my grandmother, Louise Middleton Davis Firman, who taught me to sew, and to my mother, Jacque Davis Eades, who taught me to love and appreciate antiques.

Acknowledgments

A great big thanks to everyone who has helped me during the process of writing this book. So many people have encouraged me along the way.

To my friend, author, designer, and fellow quilter Betsy Chutchian, who gave me the push to pursue my desire to write this book.

To my talented and inspiring stitch groups, who love quilting, sewing, and reproduction fabrics as much as I do and always feed my passion for creating.

To my patient and long-suffering editor, Karla Menaugh, and the fantastic C&T team, who took my ideas and transformed them into this wonderful book.

To my hard-working machine quilters, Sheri Mecom and Kerry Coburn, who took my creations and turned them into beautiful family heirlooms.

Contents

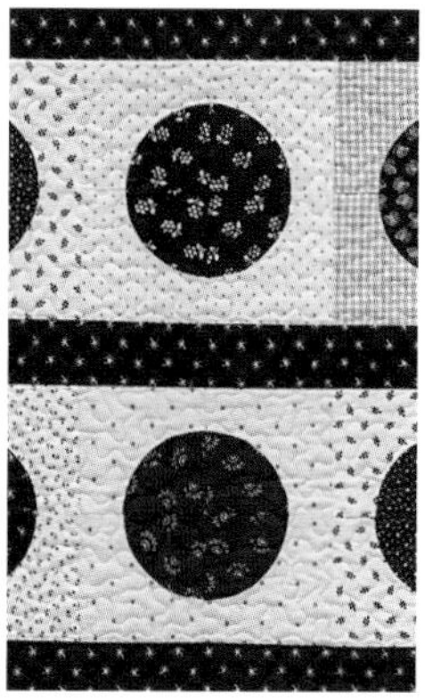

Introduction

I have a passion for quilts, and blue quilts are my favorites. Because the indigo plant has been around for centuries, the availability of its reliable and stable dye made it possible to create blue fabrics that have survived over time. The blue-and-white quilt is one of the most desirable antiques, and these quilts can still be found in good condition. This book will help you identify blue fabrics from the 1800s. Learning the characteristics of blue fabrics in the nineteenth century can help in revealing the age of an antique quilt.

Reproducing antique quilts has been made possible by wonderful, historically correct reproduction fabrics. Most fabric manufacturers feature lines of reproduction fabrics, and some lines are dated. Reproducing antique quilts can be a challenge, but it is very rewarding.

True Blue Quilts features fifteen quilt projects that represent patterns and blue fabrics found in the nineteenth century. Each chapter covers a specific time period and features the blue fabrics of that time. I hope that this book encourages you to learn a little about the history of blue fabrics and provides an inspiration for you to design and create your own heirlooms. Enjoy the projects—and always choose blue!

A Quick Blue Fabric Study Guide

Fabrics, whether antique or reproduction, will always give you hints about their age. You just need to know where to look. Here is a little information that will help you determine what period a fabric represents. If you need more guidance, there are more intensive study guides and books. I hope this information will spark your interest and inspire you to learn more.

See Resources (page 79) for a list of books about dating fabrics and a list of companies that produce reproduction fabrics.

EARLY CENTURY: 1840S AND EARLIER

During the early years in America, little fabric was produced domestically. The little fabric that was produced was locally woven, and the dyes were naturally produced. Domestic fabrics were usually used in clothing and pieced quilts, whereas imported fabrics, which mostly came from Europe or Asia, were more commonly used for bedcovers and upholstery. Indigo blues were one of the first fabrics produced in America due to the availability of indigo from farms that developed in the South. The dye from the indigo plants was relatively stable and reliable.

Europe prohibited skilled textile workers from coming to America, keeping a tight hold on fabric production in the late 1700s. Some textile workers began to immigrate secretly to America, and they brought important knowledge needed for fabric production. In 1793, Eli Whitney developed the cotton gin, a machine that separated the cotton from the seed. This made working with cotton quicker and easier. Americans began building textile mills and powered looms that helped fabric manufacturing to grow successfully and produce much more fabric in America.

Blue fabric was an early favorite. Colors that were commonly paired with blue included browns, creams, chromes, and reds.

Prints

- Roller prints, stamped prints, wovens, grounds, small figures, chintz, French toiles, large-scale prints, pillars, panels, swags, floral bouquets, flowers, geometrics, vines, serpentine stripes

Colors

- Indigo: a very dark blue
- Prussian blue: a vivid blue-green
- Lapis: a blue with a red print
- Indigo with a white or chrome print: made from a dye-resistant print stamped on the fabric before it was dyed

Examples of early blue fabrics

Block Designs

- Wholecloth, medallions, strip quilts, pieced blocks, stars, Nine-Patch, Four-Patch, squares on point, large quilts for beds

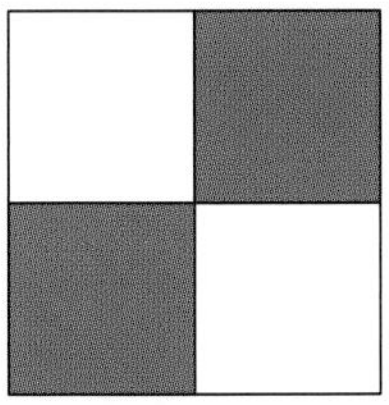

Four-Patch block

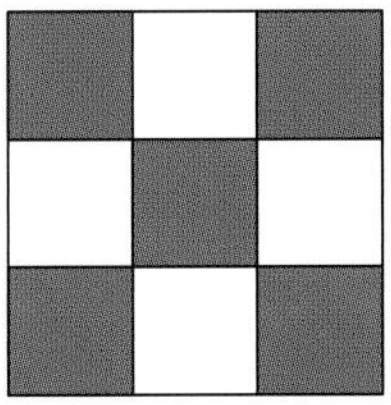

Nine-Patch block

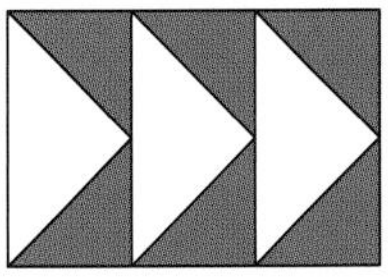

Flying Geese block

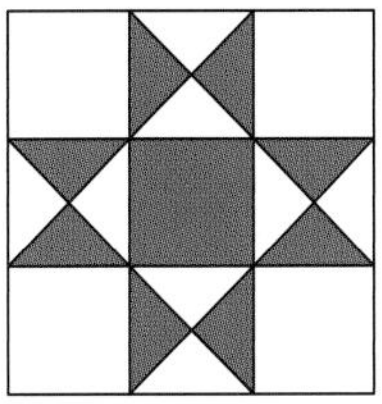

Ohio Star block

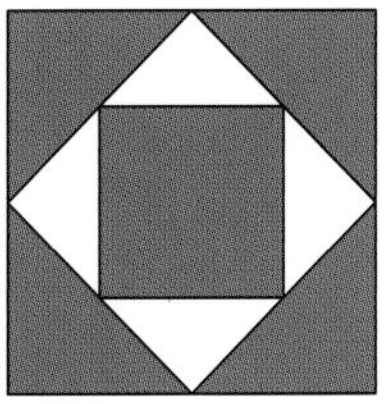

Square-in-a-Square block

Mid Century: 1840–1870

With America's independence decided, the Industrial Revolution began. The cotton gin, domestic textile mills, imported European fabrics, and the sewing machine made quiltmaking more affordable and desirable. America was still importing British and French cottons, but American textile manufacturing made fabric more easily attainable for most families. Cotton from the South was plentiful, domestic textile mills were producing fabrics, and America was growing westward.

When the American Civil War began, little fabric was produced. Any cotton grown and harvested in the South could not be sold. The Southern seaports were blockaded by the Union, so cotton could not be exported and fabrics from Europe could not be imported. Northern mills would not purchase cotton from the South because they did not want to monetarily support the South. With the fabrics they had or could obtain, Southern and Northern women were making uniforms, flags, quilts, and blankets for the soldiers. Treasured heirlooms were hidden, protecting them from being destroyed by fire, soldiers, or thieves. Some family quilts were buried with soldiers and loved ones.

Colors commonly paired with blues were green, double pink, chrome yellow, and cheddar.

Prints

- Calicos, small prints, wovens, hand-dyed cottons, small shirtings, ombrés, printed plaids

Colors

- Indigo: still a very reliable and desirable dark blue
- Prussian blue: a beautiful blue-green
- Robin's-egg blue: a soft blue
- Buff and blue: a medium blue with a buff-brown print

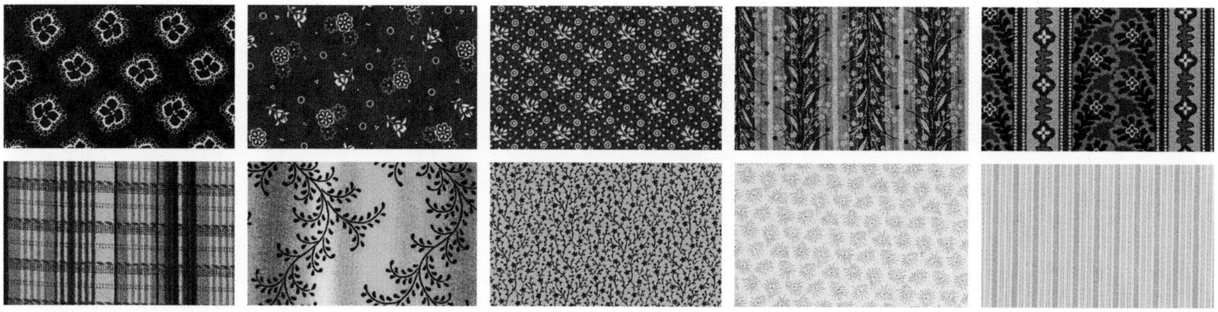

Examples of mid-century blue fabrics

Block Designs

- Appliqué, friendship blocks, blue-and-white quilts, Nine-Patch, Four-Patch, Pinwheel, Hourglass, Jacob's Ladder, Sawtooth Star, Friendship Star

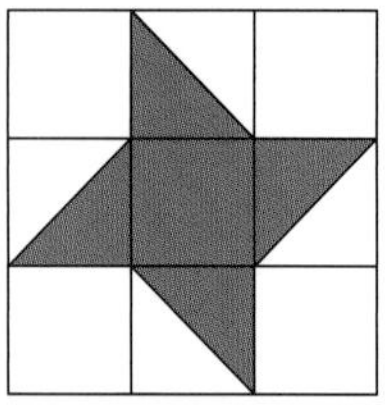

Friendship Star block

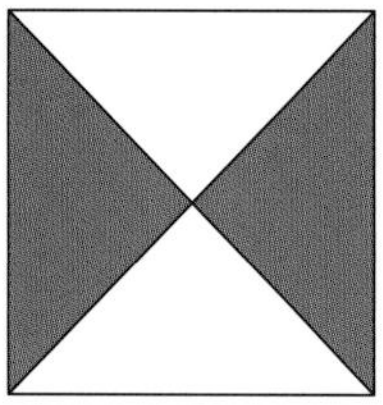

Hourglass block

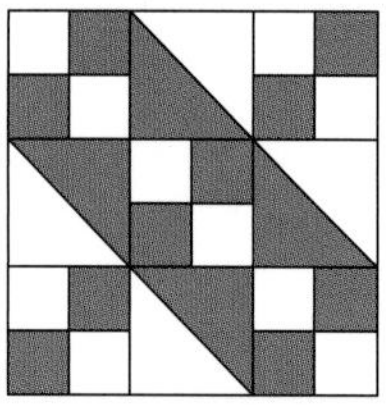

Jacob's Ladder block

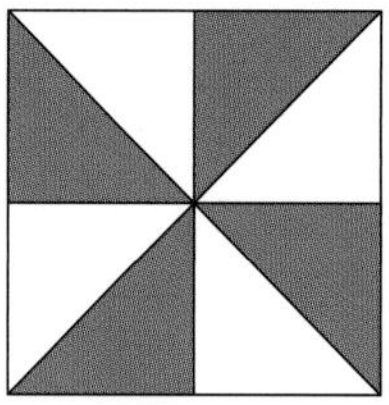

Pinwheel block

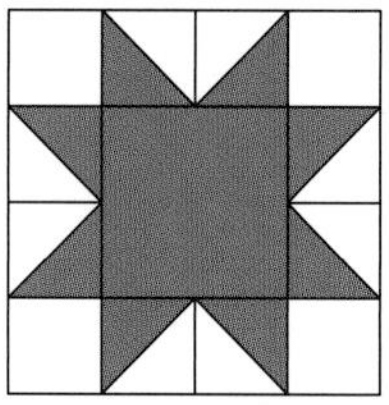

Sawtooth Star block

Late Century: 1870–1900

After the Civil War, reconstruction was necessary. In 1876 America celebrated its one-hundredth birthday. With the creation of the railroads and improvements in education and manufacturing, the nation was growing. Women were speaking out and making their own mark on society. Better education for women, the right to vote, and sobriety became supportable causes for women.

Catalogs made ready-to-wear clothes available for ordering, and that freed up women's time at home so they could become more involved in their community and the nation.

World influences had an effect on fabric designs. The 1893 World's Fair in Chicago made Americans more aware of other cultures. Japanese fabrics brought an asymmetrical style of prints that blended with the more formal European symmetrical styles.

Synthetic, colorfast dyes created an alternative to the natural dyes. The new dyes helped fabrics reliably hold their color, not fade or run. America's centennial made patriotic-themed fabrics popular, with prints including cannons, eagles, the Liberty Bell, waving flags, and political figures. The blue-and-white quilt continued its popularity during this time. Following the earlier death of Prince Albert of England in 1861, the black and gray mourning prints worn by Queen Victoria were quite the desired fashion in America.

Colors commonly used with blue were madders, greens, reds, double pinks, and purples.

Patterns

- Stripes, plaids, paisleys, calicos, shirtings, centennial prints, dots, wovens

Colors

- Indigo: still a very desirable dark blue
- Lancaster blue or double blue: a soft medium blue with a darker blue print
- Cadet blue: a medium blue with a small white print

Examples of late-century blue fabrics

Block Designs

- Feathered Star, Birds in the Air, Log Cabin, Wild Goose Chase, crazy quilts, Drunkard's Path, Bow Tie, Basket, and Bear's Paw

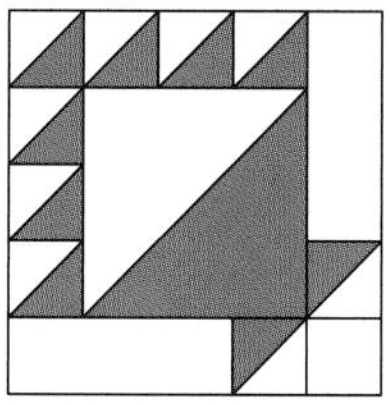

Basket block

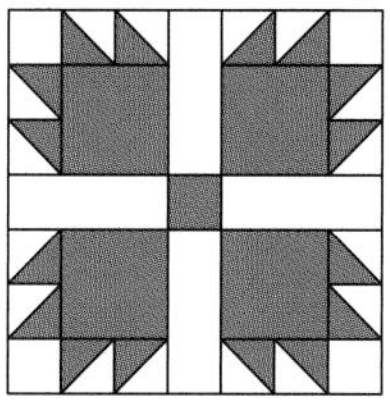

Bear's Paw block

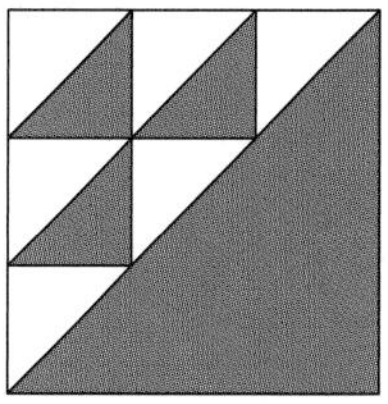

Birds in the Air block

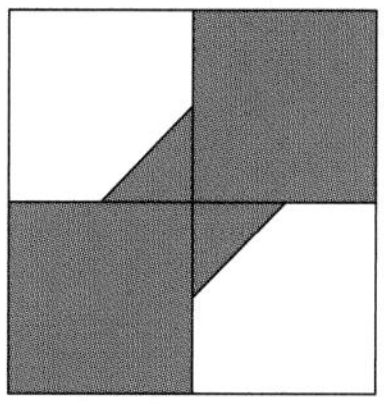

Bow Tie block

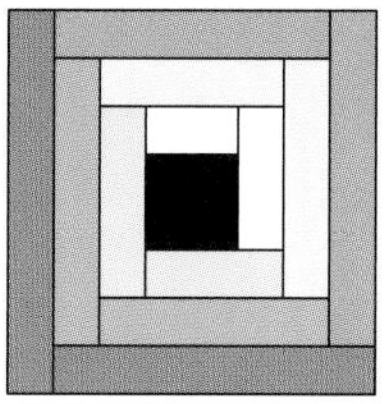

Log Cabin block

Sewing Basics

These are some of my favorite techniques for making the staples of many block patterns—half-square triangles, Flying Geese, and Hourglass blocks—as well as some of my pressing techniques. There are, however, many ways to make these popular units, and you may find other methods that work equally well or better. Use whatever technique works for you.

If you are new to quilting, I recommend taking a class at your local quilt shop or searching online to learn more about basic rotary-cutting and quiltmaking techniques. A good resource is C&T Publishing's Quiltmaking Basics (refer to ctpub.com > scroll down to Support: Quiltmaking Basics & Sewing Tips).

Making Half-Square Triangles

Refer to the project instructions for the size of the squares. This method makes 2 half-square triangles at a time. See Making Many Half-Square Triangles (below) for information about making more than 2 blocks at a time.

1. Pair 2 squares with right sides together. Lightly draw a diagonal line from one corner to the opposite corner on the wrong side of 1 square.

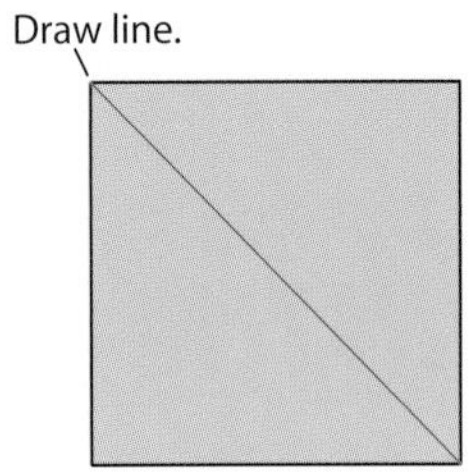

2. Sew a scant ¼″ seam on each side of the line. Cut on the drawn line.

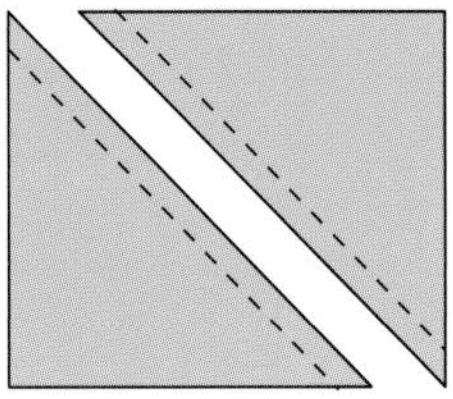

4. Press, and trim off the dog-ears. Trim to size if needed.

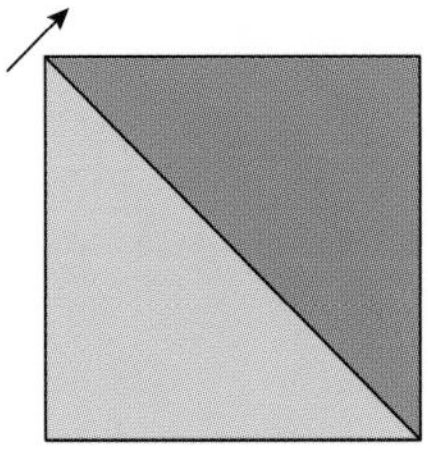

Tip

Making Many Half-Square Triangles

Many quilts use half-square triangles. If you need to make several (or a lot!) of half-square triangles in a single color combination, you may want to use triangle papers. These papers contain a grid of sewing and cutting lines for making multiple half-square triangles from large cuts of fabric. They are easy to use, include simple directions, and are offered by many different brands on the market. I commonly use triangle papers; if you have never used them, I would encourage you to give them a try.

Making Hourglass Blocks

These also are called quarter-square triangles. Refer to the project instructions for the size of the squares. This method makes 2 Hourglass blocks at a time.

1. Pair 2 squares with right sides together. Lightly draw a diagonal line from one corner to the opposite corner on the wrong side of 1 square.

2. Sew a scant ¼″ seam on each side of the line. Before cutting on the drawn line, draw another line on the opposite diagonal, corner to corner. Cut apart on both lines, yielding 4 pieces.

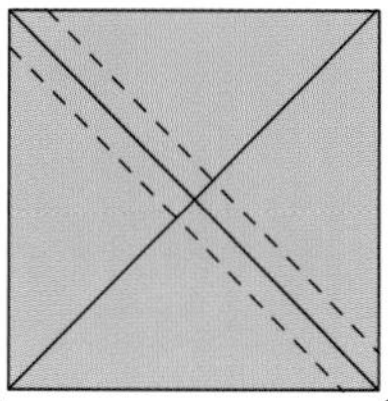

3. Press each triangle open. Place 2 triangles right sides together, with like colors at opposite ends. Let the seams nest for easy matching. Sew together and press open.

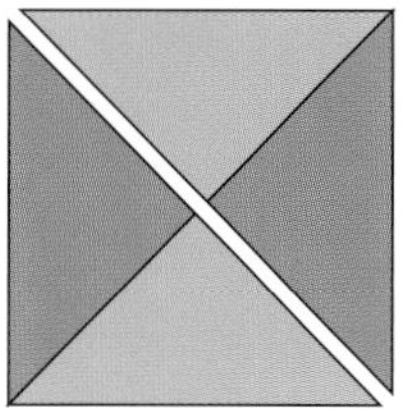

4. Square up the quarter-square triangles to the desired size.

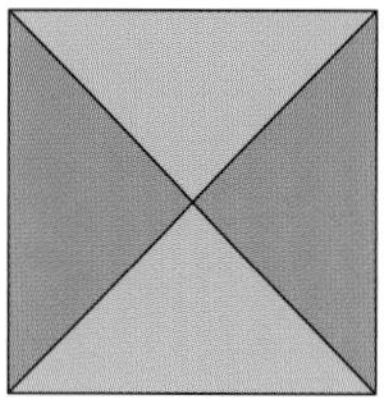

Making Flying Geese

Refer to the project instructions for the size of the squares and rectangle.

1. Lightly draw a diagonal line from one corner to the opposite corner on the wrong side of 2 squares.

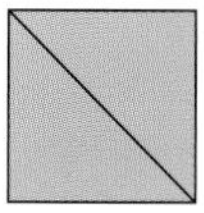

2. With right sides together, place a square on one end of the rectangle. Sew directly on the line, trim the seam allowance to ¼″, and press open.

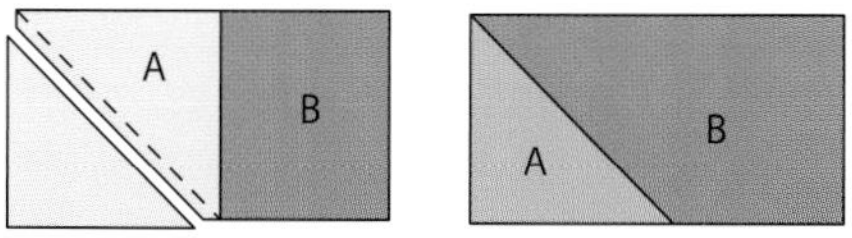

3. With right sides together, place the other square on the other end of the rectangle. Sew directly on the line, trim the seam allowance to ¼″, and press open. Trim to size if needed.

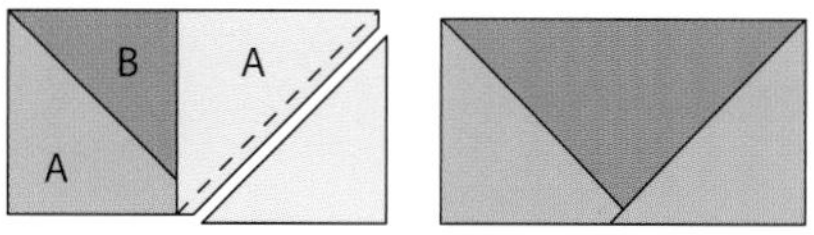

Pressing Tip: The Clip Trick

When you sew blocks together that result in bulky intersections, as in *Westward Ships* (page 64), the seams may not want to lie flat. Use this tip when pressing these blocks. The seam allowances will nest nicely, reducing bulk.

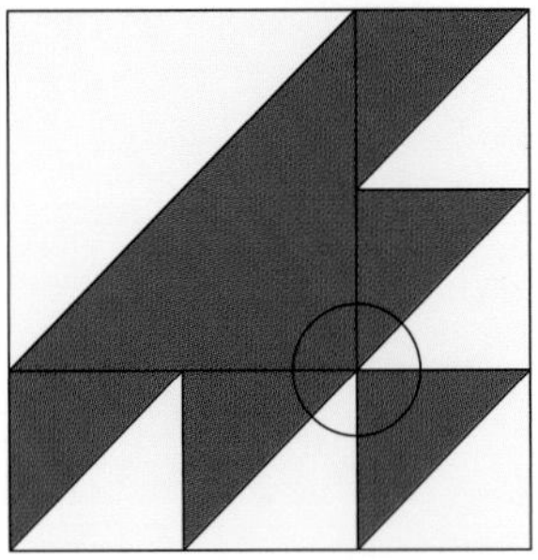

Blocks with a lot of triangles, such as Lost Ship, have bulky seam allowances that are hard to press.

1. In each block, clip ¼″ on either side of the seam.

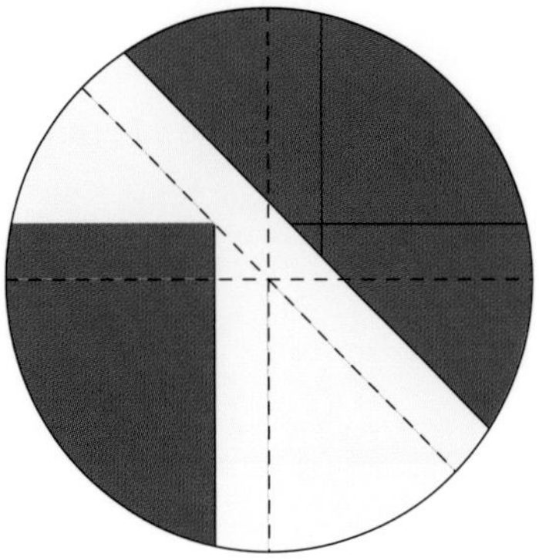

2. Press the clipped intersection open, and then press the other seam allowances toward the darker fabric.

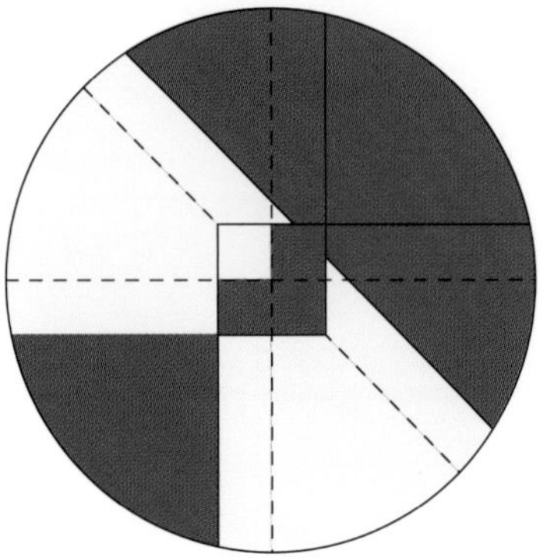

Finishing Your Quilt

Backing

Plan on making the backing a minimum of 8″ longer and wider than the quilt top. Piece if necessary. Trim the selvages before you piece to the desired size.

To economize, piece the back from any leftover quilting fabrics or blocks in your collection.

Batting

The type of batting to use is a personal decision; consult your local quilt shop. Cut batting approximately 8″ longer and wider than your quilt top. Note that your batting choice will affect how much quilting is necessary for the quilt. Check the manufacturer's instructions to see how far apart the quilting lines can be.

Layering

Spread the backing wrong side up and tape the edges down with masking tape. (If you are working on carpet, you can use T-pins to secure the backing to the carpet.) Center the batting on top, smoothing out any folds. Place the quilt top, right side up, on top of the batting and backing, making sure it is centered.

Basting

Basting keeps the quilt "sandwich" layers from shifting while you are quilting. If you plan to machine quilt, pin baste the quilt layers together with safety pins placed about 3″–4″ apart. Begin basting in the center and move toward the edges, first in vertical rows, then in horizontal rows. Try not to pin directly on the intended quilting lines.

If you plan to hand quilt, baste the layers together with thread, using a long needle and light-colored thread. Knot one end of the thread. Using stitches approximately the length of the needle, begin in the center and move out toward the edges in vertical and horizontal rows approximately 4″ apart. Add two diagonal rows of basting.

Quilting

Quilting, whether by hand or machine, enhances the pieced or appliquéd design of the quilt. You may choose to quilt-in-the-ditch, echo the pieced or appliquéd motifs, use patterns from quilting design books and stencils, or do your own free-motion quilting. Remember to check your batting manufacturer's recommendations for how close together the quilting lines must be.

Binding

Trim excess batting and backing from the quilt, making them even with the edges of the quilt top.

Double-Fold Straight-Grain Binding

If you want a ¼″ finished binding, cut the binding strips 1⅝″ wide and piece them together with diagonal seams to make a continuous binding strip. Trim the seam allowances to ¼″. Press the seams open.

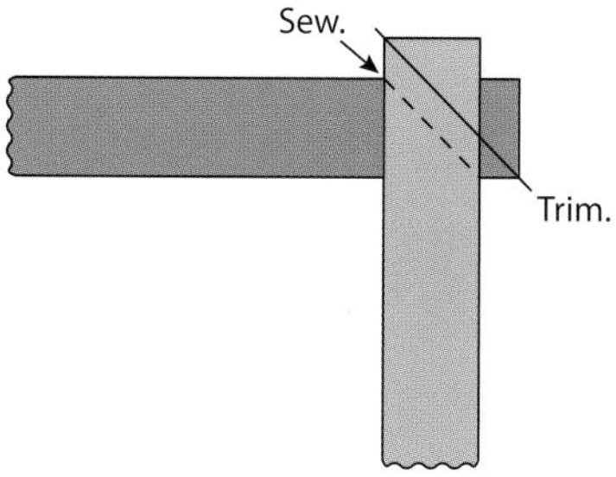

Sew from corner to corner.

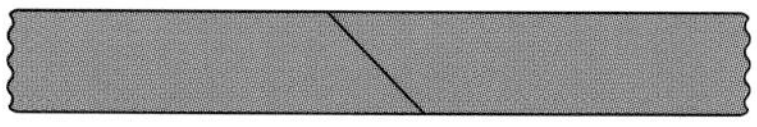

Completed diagonal seam

Press the entire strip in half lengthwise, with wrong sides together. With raw edges even, pin the binding to the front edge of the quilt a few inches away from a corner, leaving the first few inches of the binding unattached. Start sewing, using a ¼″ seam allowance.

Stop ¼″ away from the first corner (Step 1), and backstitch one stitch. Lift the presser foot and needle. Rotate the quilt one-quarter turn. Fold the binding at a right angle so it extends straight above the quilt and the fold forms a 45° angle in the corner (Step 2). Then bring the binding strip down even with the edge of the quilt (Step 3). Begin sewing at the folded edge. Repeat in the same manner at all corners.

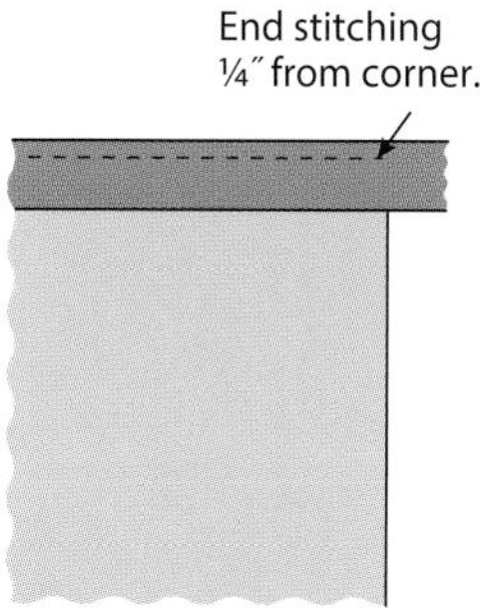

Step 1. Stitch to ¼″ from the corner.

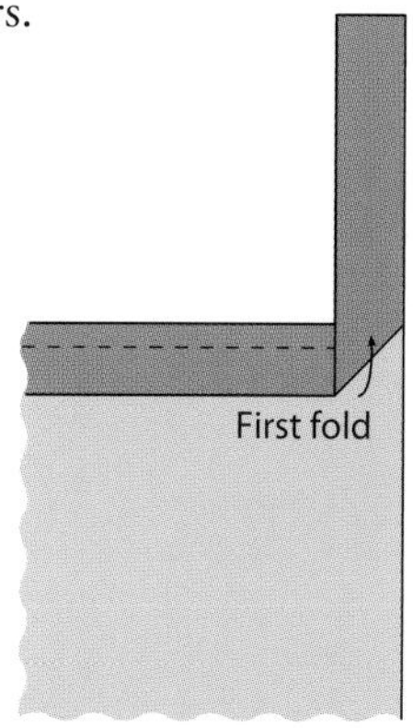

Step 2. First fold for the miter

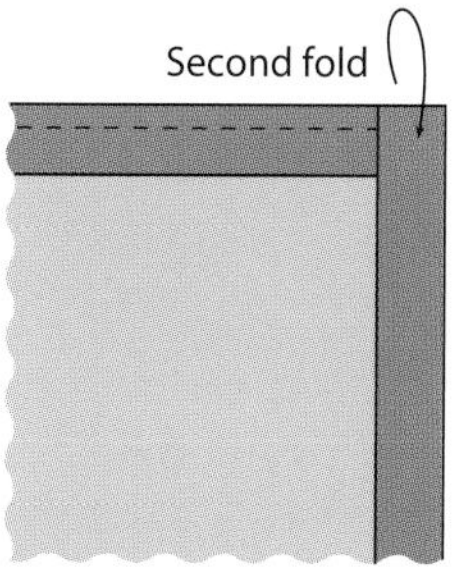

Step 3. Second fold alignment

Continue stitching until you are back near the beginning of the binding strip. See Finishing the Binding Ends (page 16) for tips on finishing and hiding the raw edges of the binding ends.

Finishing the Binding Ends

METHOD 1

After stitching around the quilt, fold under the beginning tail of the binding strip ¼″ so that the raw edge will be inside the binding after it is turned to the back of the quilt. Place the end tail of the binding strip over the beginning folded end. Continue to attach the binding and stitch slightly beyond the starting stitches. Trim the excess binding. Fold the binding over the raw edges to the quilt back and hand stitch, mitering the corners.

METHOD 2

Refer to ctpub.com > scroll down to Support: Quiltmaking Basics & Sewing Tips > Completing a Binding With an Invisible Seam. Fold the ending tail of the binding back on itself where it meets the beginning binding tail. From the fold, measure and mark the cut width of your binding strip. Cut the ending binding tail to this measurement. For example, if your binding is cut 1⅝″ wide, measure from the fold on the ending tail of the binding 1⅝″ and cut the binding tail to this length.

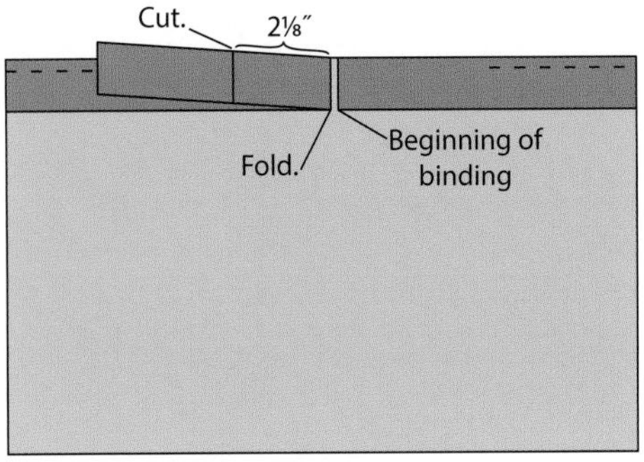

Cut the binding tail.

Open both tails. Place one tail on top of the other tail at right angles, right sides together. Mark a diagonal line from corner to corner and stitch on the line. Check that you've done it correctly and that the binding fits the quilt; then trim the seam allowance to ¼″. Press open.

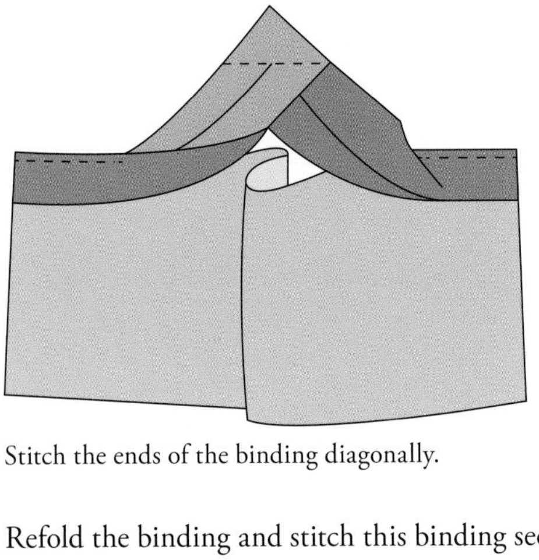

Stitch the ends of the binding diagonally.

Refold the binding and stitch this binding section in place on the quilt. Fold the binding over the raw edges to the quilt back and hand stitch.

Early Blue Projects: 1840 and Earlier

Early blue quilts were generally made using simple blocks and large prints. The blues you would see in antique quilts from this period could be indigos, bright Prussian blues, or softer blues. Many antique quilts of this period feature soft browns to complement the blues. There were also appliqué quilts during this period, along with wholecloth quilts.

Designed and made by Annette Plog, quilted by Sheri Mecom

Prussian Blue Four-Patch

Finished quilt: 68″ × 79″ • **Finished block:** 4″ × 4″

This quilt is my reproduction of a wonderful antique quilt dated 1830. I used Prussian blues and browns in florals, stripes, ombrés, and different-sized prints. Although the quilt is assembled in diagonal rows, the alternate blocks form strong vertical lines at the center and then surround and frame the quilt.

Materials

Lights, mediums, and darks: ¼ yard each of 18 different browns, tans, and blues

Medium tan floral: ⅝ yard

Medium blue floral: ¾ yard

Light floral: ¾ yard

Dark brown: ⅞ yard

Setting triangles: ¾ yard of light blue

Binding: ½ yard

Backing: 5 yards

Batting: 76″ × 87″

Cutting

Four-Patch blocks

From *each* of the 18 lights, mediums, and darks:

- Cut 3 strips 2½″ × width of fabric.

Alternate blocks

Medium tan floral

- Cut 4 strips 4½″ × width of fabric.

  Subcut 27 squares 4½″ × 4½″.

Medium blue floral

- Cut 5 strips 4½″ × width of fabric.

  Subcut 36 squares 4½″ × 4½″.

Light floral

- Cut 5 strips 4½″ × width of fabric.

  Subcut 36 squares 4½″ × 4½″.

Dark brown

- Cut 6 strips 4½″ × width of fabric.

  Subcut 44 squares 4½″ × 4½″.

Setting triangles

- Cut 12 squares 7″ × 7″. Cut each square in quarters diagonally to yield 48 side setting triangles.

- Cut 2 squares 3¾″ × 3¾″. Cut each square in half diagonally to yield 4 corner setting triangles.

CONSTRUCTION

Four-Patch Block

Work with pairs of 2½″ strips from the light, medium, and dark fabrics, making sure there is some contrast between the strips in each pair. The strips don't have to contrast a lot. Some pairs should have strong contrast, while others could contain different colors of similar value.

1. Right sides together, stitch the strips along the long edge. Press the seam allowance toward the darker fabric.

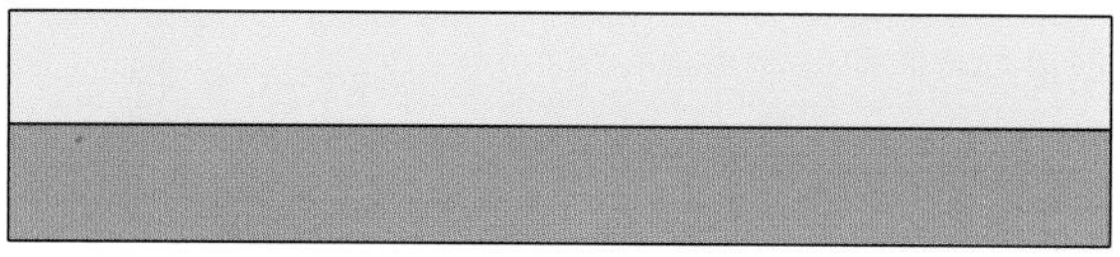

2. Cut the strip set into 14 segments 2½″ wide.

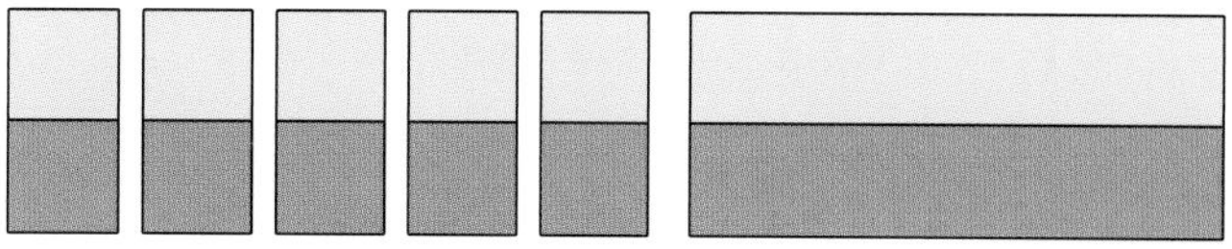

3. Place a pair of segments right sides together, with like colors at opposite ends. Sew together and press the seam to one side to complete a Four-Patch block.

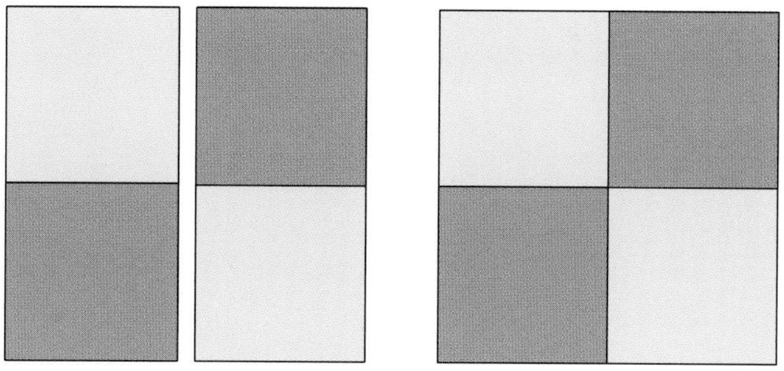

Four-Patch block. Make 168.

4. Repeat Steps 1–3, using all of the light, medium, and dark 2½″ strips to make 168 blocks. There will be extra segments.

Quilt Assembly

1. Referring to the quilt photo for color placement and to the quilt assembly diagram (next page), arrange the Four-Patch blocks, alternate blocks, side setting triangles, and corner setting triangles in diagonal rows.

NOTE Step-by-Step Block Placement

It may be easier for you to understand the block placement if you start by arranging all of the alternate blocks first and then fill in the open spaces with the Four-Patch blocks. Arrange the alternate blocks on point, tip to tip.

1. Starting in the center of the quilt, place a column of 9 tan floral alternate blocks on point.

2. Place a column of 9 blue floral alternate blocks on each side of the tan column.

3. Add another column of 9 tan floral blocks on each side of the blue blocks and then another column of 9 blue floral blocks on the outside edges. This completes the vertical columns of alternate blocks at the quilt center.

4. Next create an inner border of light floral blocks around the vertical columns. Start by placing a column of 9 light floral blocks on each side of the blue columns. Then place a row of 9 light floral blocks across the top and bottom of the quilt.

5. In the same manner as in Step 4, create an outer border of dark brown blocks around the quilt.

6. Fill in with Four-Patch blocks in all the open spaces. Place most of the Four-Patches with the brown patches in the horizontal positions, but mix it up every now and then to add a random quality to the placement.

2. Sew the quilt together in diagonal rows, starting at the top left corner. Sew the rows together to complete the top.

Quilt assembly

Finishing

Quilt using a favorite quilt design. This one is machine quilted with an overall orange peel design. Follow Finishing Your Quilt (page 14) to bind your quilt, and enjoy.

Designed and made by Annette Plog, quilted by Sheri Mecom

Strippy Hourglass

Finished quilt: 66″ × 72″ • **Finished block:** 6″ × 6″

Because this quilt uses two larger blocks set in columns and separated by a floral fabric, it is a good quilt for featuring large-print fabrics. The larger blocks let you highlight plaids, stripes, and bold fabrics, while the separating strips may be made with beautiful florals, chintzes, and fussy-cut stripes. Be creative and be bold!

I used less contrast in the Nine-Patch blocks, which lets the Hourglass blocks attract the most attention. You can play with the contrast for other looks. The wonderful vertical sashing fabric I used was Rue Indienne by French General for Moda Fabrics.

Materials

For the blocks, choose early blue fabrics, such as indigos, Prussian blues, and indigo-with-white prints.

Lights: ¾ yard each of 3 different lights

Mediums: ¾ yard each of 3 different mediums

Darks: ¾ yard each of 3 different darks

Vertical sashing: 2⅛ yards

Binding: ½ yard

Backing: 4½ yards

Batting: 74″ × 80″

Cutting

Hourglass blocks

Hourglass block

Use the same color combinations for each set of columns.

- Cut 6 light and 6 dark squares 7½″ × 7½″ for Columns 1 and 5.
- Cut 6 light and 6 dark squares 7½″ × 7½″ for Columns 2 and 4.
- Cut 3 light and 3 dark squares 7½″ × 7½″ for Column 3.

Nine-Patch blocks

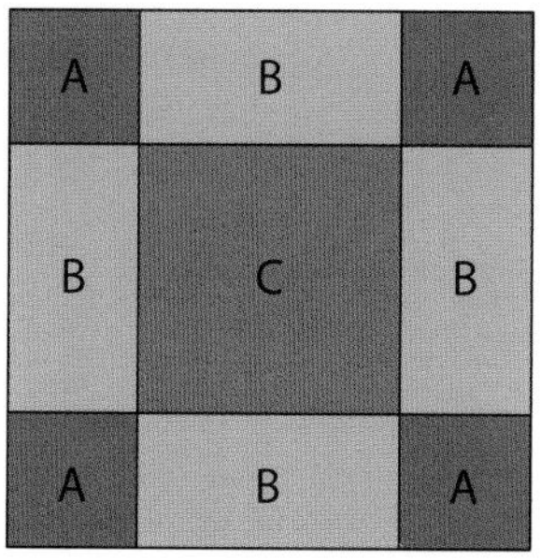

Nine-Patch block

Use the same color combinations for each set of columns.

Columns 1 and 5

From a dark fabric:

- Cut 48 squares 2″ × 2″ for piece A.
- Cut 12 squares 3½″ × 3½″ for piece C.

From a light or medium fabric:

- Cut 48 rectangles 2″ × 3½″ for piece B.

Columns 2 and 4

From a dark fabric:

- Cut 48 squares 2″ × 2″ for piece A.
- Cut 12 squares 3½″ × 3½″ for piece C.

From a light or medium fabric:

- Cut 48 rectangles 2″ × 3½″ for piece B.

Column 3

From a dark fabric:

- Cut 24 squares 2″ × 2″ for piece A.
- Cut 6 squares 3½″ × 3½″ for piece C.

From a light or medium fabric:

- Cut 24 rectangles 2″ × 3½″ for piece B.

Vertical sashing

- On the *length* of the fabric, cut 6 strips 6½″ × 72½″.

You may want to cut your strips a little longer in case your quilt turns out to be a slightly different size from the pattern. You can trim the sashing strips after you have assembled the columns of Hourglass and Nine-Patch blocks.

> **Tip**
>
> **Cutting Sashing Strips with Border Print Fabric**
>
> If you find a great columnar print for sashing, you may want to fussy cut the strips to highlight the design in your fabric. If you fussy cut the sashing, the width will depend on the design in the fabric.

Construction

Hourglass Block

Refer to Making Hourglass Blocks (page 13) for sewing instructions. Use the 7½" × 7½" light and dark squares to make blocks that measure 6½" × 6½".

1. Using the 6 light and 6 dark squares, make 12 Hourglass blocks for Columns 1 and 5.

2. Using the second set of 6 light and 6 dark squares in another color combination, make 12 more Hourglass blocks for Columns 2 and 4.

3. Using the remaining 3 light and 3 dark squares, make 6 Hourglass blocks for Column 3.

Nine-Patch Block

For each block, choose 4 matching A squares, 4 matching B rectangles, and 1 C square. The block should measure 6½" × 6½".

1. Sew an A square to each end of a B rectangle. Make 2.

2. Sew a B rectangle to 2 opposite sides of a C square.

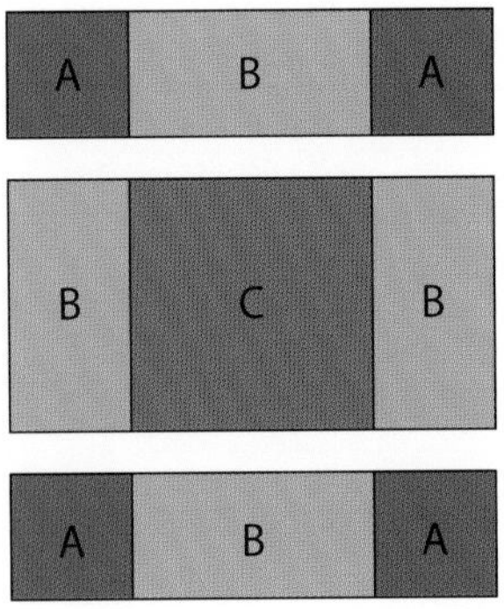

3. Sew a unit from Step 1 to the top and bottom of the unit from Step 2 to complete the Nine-Patch block. The block should measure 6½" × 6½".

4. Using fabrics in the same color combination, repeat Steps 1–3 to make a total of 12 blocks for Columns 1 and 5.

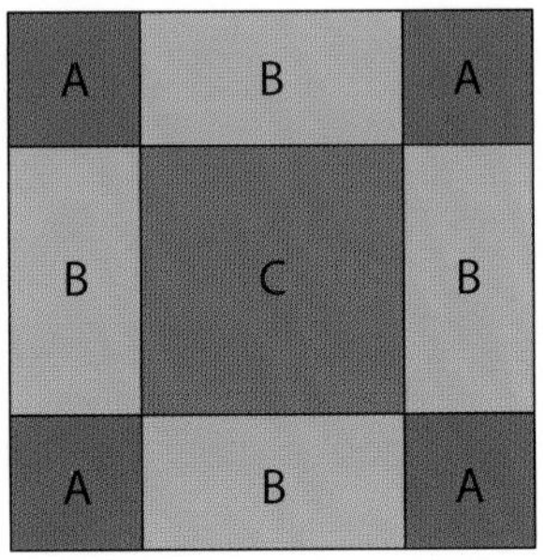

Nine-Patch block

5. Using fabrics in a second color combination, repeat Steps 1–3 to make a total of 12 blocks for Columns 2 and 4.

6. Using fabrics in a third color combination, repeat Steps 1–3 to make a total of 6 blocks for Column 3.

Quilt Assembly

1. Referring to the quilt assembly diagram (below), arrange the blocks in columns. Alternate Hourglass blocks and Nine-Patch blocks, starting with an Hourglass block at the top and ending with a Nine-Patch block. Pay special attention to placing the color combinations in the correct column. Sew the blocks in each column together. Each column should measure 6½″ × 72½″.

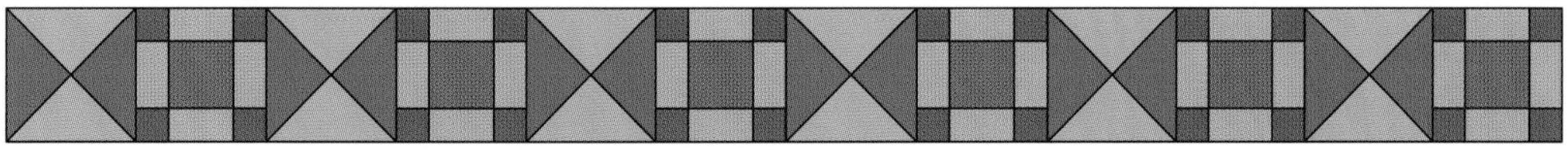

2. Place a sashing strip between each pieced column and on each outer edge of the quilt.

3. Sew the columns together to complete the top.

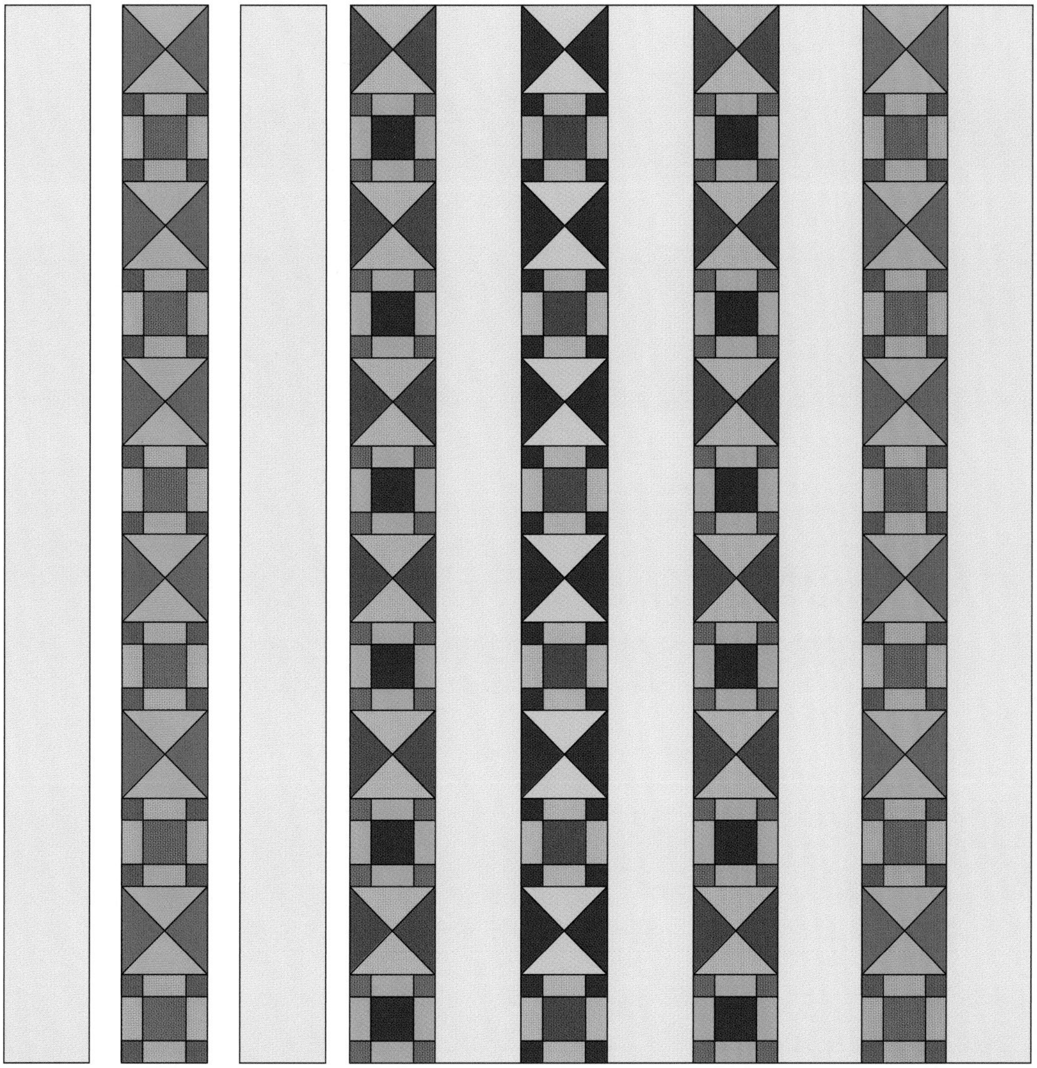

Quilt assembly

Finishing

Quilt using a favorite quilt design. This one is machine quilted using an overall clamshell design. Follow Finishing Your Quilt (page 14) to bind your quilt, and enjoy.

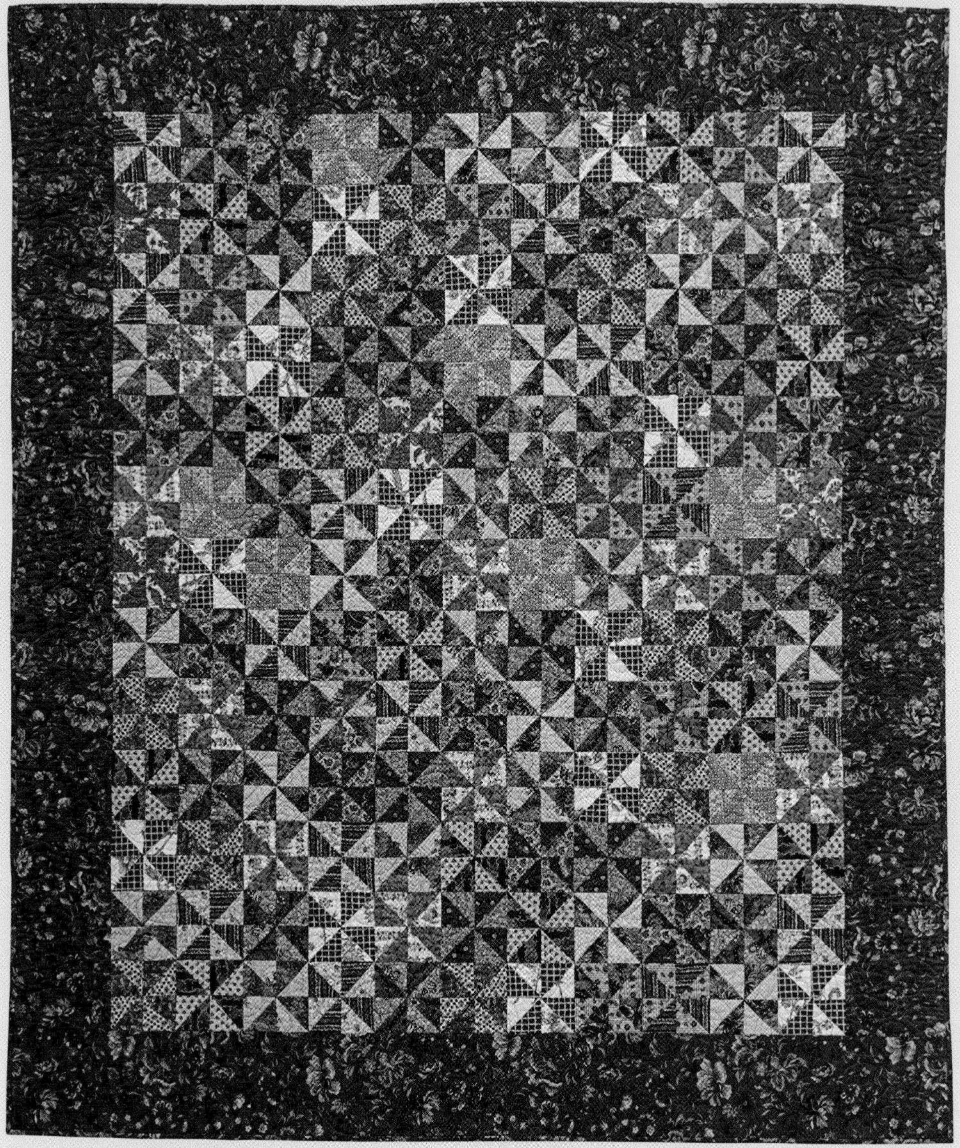

Designed and made by Annette Plog, quilted by Sheri Mecom

Colonial Pinwheels

Finished quilt: 56″ × 64″ • **Finished block:** 4″ × 4″

The Pinwheel block was a favorite in early quilts. This block allowed the quilter to use scraps, and it was easy enough for a beginner or young quilter to make. When you want a scrappy look, use many different medium and dark fabrics for the darker fabric and different shades of light fabrics for the light. Don't be afraid to use white fabrics—they make the quilt sparkle.

The border is a great place to show off one of your large floral favorites. The one I used is from a line of fabric called Eliza's Indigo. It was designed by Betsy Chutchian for Moda Fabrics. Just beautiful!

Materials

Lights, mediums, and darks: ¼ yard each of 24 different browns, tans, and blues

Border: 1¾ yards of blue floral

Binding: ½ yard

Backing: 3¾ yards

Batting: 64″ × 72″

Cutting

Pinwheel blocks

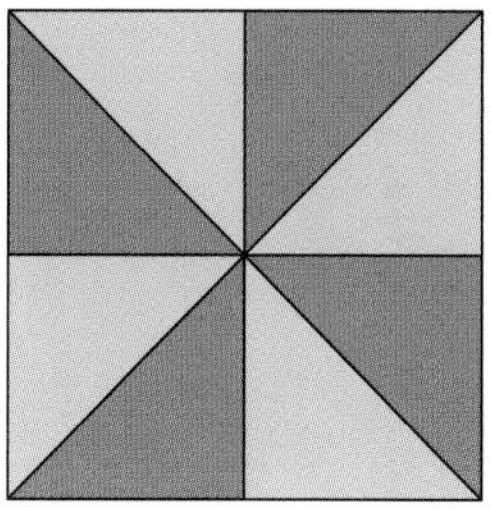

Pinwheel block

The following directions are for making the half-square triangles 2 at a time. If you would rather use half-square triangle papers to make more half-square triangles at once, read the instructions for the papers before you cut the pinwheel fabric.

From *each* of the 24 lights, mediums, and darks:

- Cut 2 strips 3″ × width of fabric.

  Sort the strips into pairs of contrasting fabrics. Stack the strips and subcut 12 squares 3″ × 3″ from each strip set. Keep the pairs of squares together.

Border

On the *length* of the fabric:

- Cut 2 strips 6½″ × 52½″ for each side border.
- Cut 2 strips 6½″ × 56½″ for the top and bottom border.

NOTE You may want to cut your strips a little longer in case your quilt turns out to be a slightly different size from the pattern. You may trim them after you have assembled the Pinwheel blocks.

Construction

Pinwheel Block

1. Refer to Making Half-Square Triangles (page 12) for sewing instructions. From a set of paired fabrics, use the 3″ × 3″ squares to make 24 half-square triangles measuring 2½″ × 2½″.

2. Repeat Step 1 to make 24 half-square triangles from each set of paired fabrics, 576 total.

Tip

Making Many Half-Square Triangles

For quilts like this one, for which you need to make 24 half-square triangles from the same set of fabrics, try using one of the printed papers designed specifically for half-square triangles. These papers contain grids of squares marked with diagonal cutting and sewing lines, allowing you to start with larger sections of fabric and make more than 2 half-square triangles at a time. These products can make the process quick and easy.

The brands of paper vary, and you will need to cut your fabric specifically for your chosen product. If you plan to use half-square triangle paper, remember to read the directions before cutting your fabric for half-square triangles. For this project you will need the size for 2″ finished half-square triangles.

3. Arrange 4 matching half-square triangles in a pinwheel. Sew the top 2 squares together and then the bottom 2 squares together. Sew the rows together to complete the block. Press the block as desired, but remember to press all the blocks the same way. The block should measure 4½″ × 4½″.

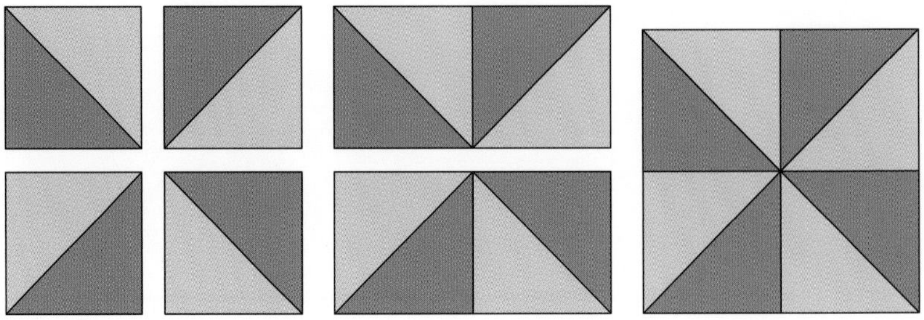

4. Repeat Step 3 to make 143 Pinwheel blocks. There will be extra half-square triangles.

Quilt Assembly

1. Referring to the quilt photo for color placement and to the quilt assembly diagram (next page), arrange the Pinwheels in 13 rows of 11 blocks each. Take some time to place the different colors in an arrangement that pleases you.

2. Sew together 1 row at a time, and then sew the rows together. Your quilt top should measure 44½″ × 52½″.

3. Sew a 6½″ × 52½″ border strip to each side of the quilt top. Press the seam allowance toward the border. Sew a 6½″ × 56½″ border strip to the top and bottom of the quilt to complete the top.

Finishing

Quilt using a favorite quilt design. This one is machine quilted using an overall graphic design. Follow Finishing Your Quilt (page 14) to bind your quilt, and enjoy.

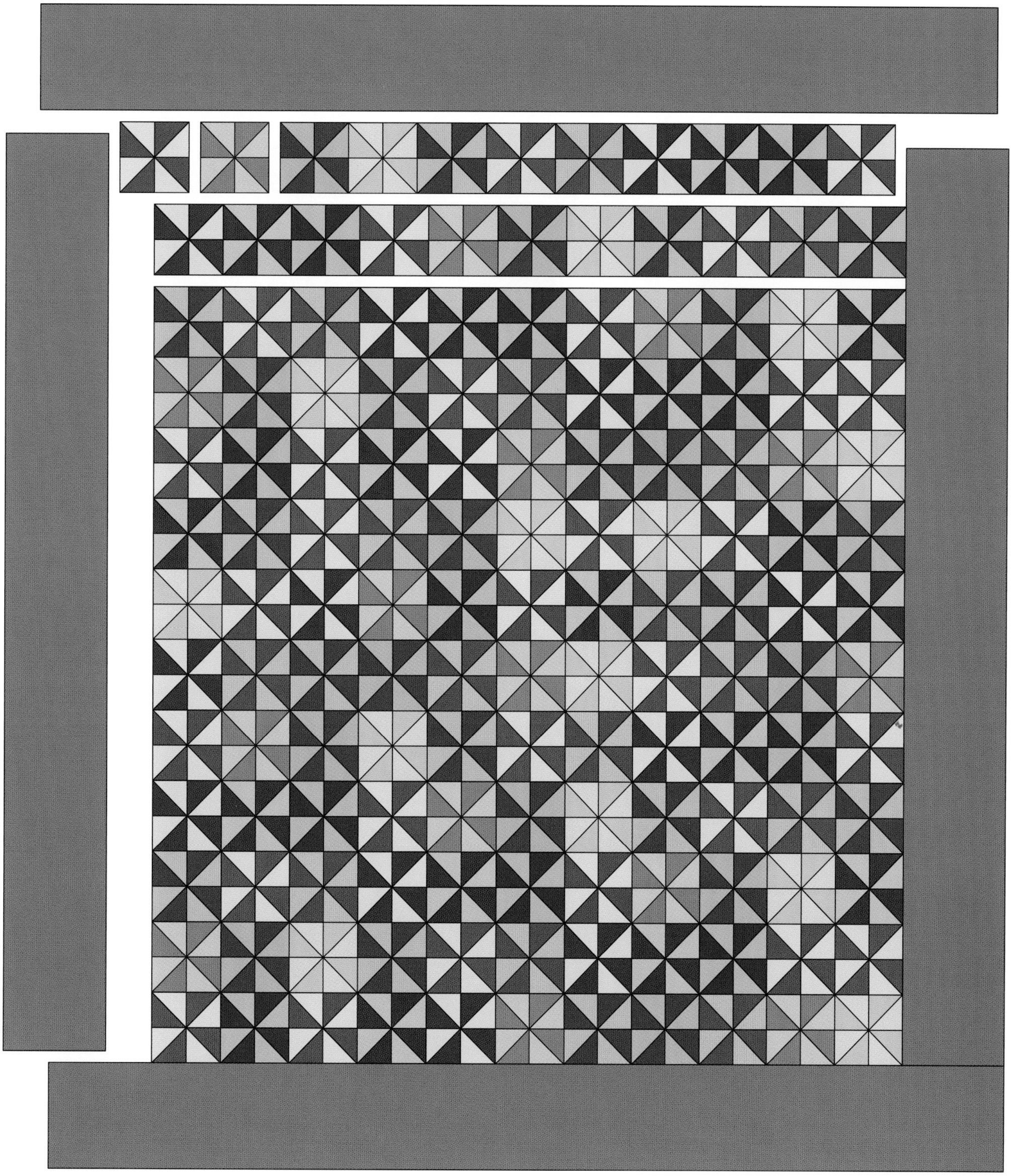

Quilt assembly

Designed, made, and quilted by Annette Plog

Indigo Lane

Finished quilt: 24″ × 30″ • **Finished block:** 4″ × 4″

Four-Patch blocks and squares combine to make Double Four-Patch blocks in this quilt. Arranged to create diagonal stripes, they create a striking, bold design. This design is traditional, but the use of contrasting light and dark fabrics can give it a contemporary feel. Using fabrics that blend together would create a softer quilt with a less distinct design.

Many of the early dark indigos in this quilt are from a reproduction fabric line called Dargate Polychromes by designer and historian Margo Krager for Andover Fabrics. They have a bright and vivid print. One of the prints in the large squares is a floral with a mostly solid stripe, which makes it look like I pieced some of the squares. A nice optical illusion!

Materials

Indigo blue: ⅛ yard each of 5 or more different fabrics

Lights: ⅛ yard each of 5 or more different fabrics

Border and binding: ⅝ yard of indigo blue

Backing: 1 yard

Batting: 28″ × 34″

Cutting

Double Four-Patch blocks

Dark Double Four-Patch block

Light Double Four-Patch block

From *each* of the 5 indigo blues and 5 lights:

- Cut 1 strip 2½″ × width of fabric.

  From each strip, subcut 7 squares 2½″ × 2½″ for the alternate squares. You will have a few squares left over, but the extras will give you some flexibility in arranging the colors.

- Cut 1 strip 1½″ × width of fabric for the Four-Patch strip sets.

Border

You may want to wait to cut your borders in case your quilt turns out to be a slightly different size from the pattern.

- Cut 2 strips 2½″ × 26½″ for the side borders.
- Cut 2 strips 2½″ × 24½″ for the top and bottom borders.

Construction

Double Four-Patch Block

1. Place a blue 1½″ strip and a light 1½″ strip right sides together and stitch along a long edge. Press the seam allowance toward the dark fabric.

2. Cut the strip set into 1½″ segments.

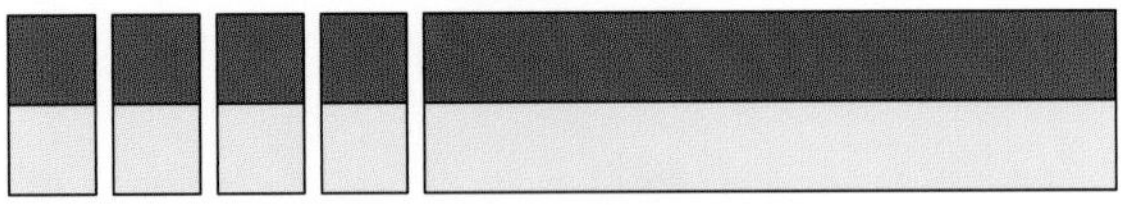

3. Repeat Steps 1 and 2 with the remaining pairs of blue and light strips.

4. Pair 2 segments of different color combinations from Steps 2 and 3, and sew them together to make a four-patch unit. This unit should measure 2½″ × 2½″.

5. Repeat Step 4 to make a total of 65 units.

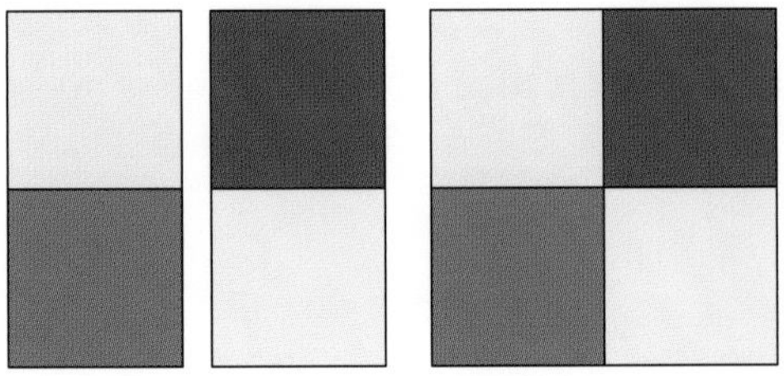

6. Arrange 2 blue 2½″ × 2½″ squares and 2 Four-Patch blocks, with the blue squares in opposite corners. Sew the top 2 squares together and then the bottom 2 squares together. Sew the rows together to complete the block. Make 15.

Dark Double Four-Patch block. Make 15.

7. Repeat Step 6, using 2 light 2½″ × 2½″ squares in place of the blue squares. Make 15.

Light Double Four-Patch block. Make 15.

Quilt Assembly

1. The top row is made from 5 Four-Patch blocks, 3 blue 2½″ × 2½″ squares, and 2 light 2½″ × 2½″ squares. Referring to the quilt assembly diagram (below), arrange the blocks in the top row.

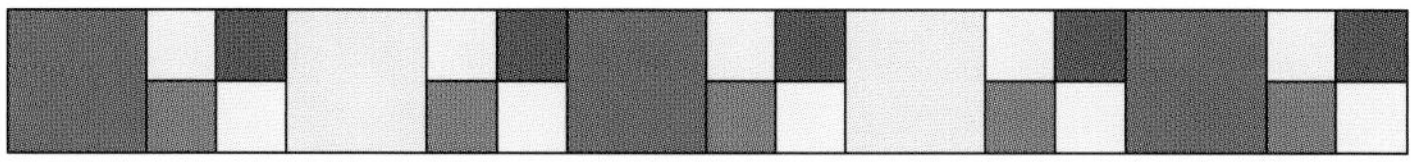

2. Refer to the quilt assembly diagram to arrange the Double Four-Patch blocks in 6 rows of 5 blocks each. Alternate dark and light blocks, starting with a light block at the left edge of the second row.

3. Sew the blocks in each row together, and then sew the rows together. Your top should measure 20½″ × 26½″.

4. Measure your top to check the size. If it is different than the pattern size, trim your border strips to fit.

5. Sew a 2½″ × 26½″ border strip to each side of the quilt top. Press the seam allowance toward the border. Sew a 2½″ × 24½″ border strip to the top and bottom of the quilt to complete the top.

Quilt assembly

Finishing

Quilt using a favorite quilt design. This one is machine quilted using an overall grid design. Follow Finishing Your Quilt (page 14) to bind your quilt, and enjoy.

Designed, made, and quilted by Annette Plog

Cambridge Table Square

Finished table square: 30″ × 30″ • **Finished block:** 4″ × 4″

Sometimes a fabric is chosen before a quilt is designed. I wanted to feature this beautiful floral indigo, so I designed this sweet table square with the fabric in mind. The large floral is from Betsy Chutchian's fabric line called Eliza's Indigo for Moda Fabrics. This quilt is made with 4″ Sawtooth Stars and scrappy 1″ half-square triangles. The border is large enough to highlight the wonderful floral fabric. Let this simple quilt feature one of your treasured fabrics.

Materials

Blues and indigos: 6 or more fat eighths *or* ⅛ yards

Lights: 2 or more fat quarters *or* ¼ yards

Alternate blocks, border, binding, and backing: 2⅛ yards of dark blue

Batting: 34″ × 34″

Cutting

Sawtooth Star blocks

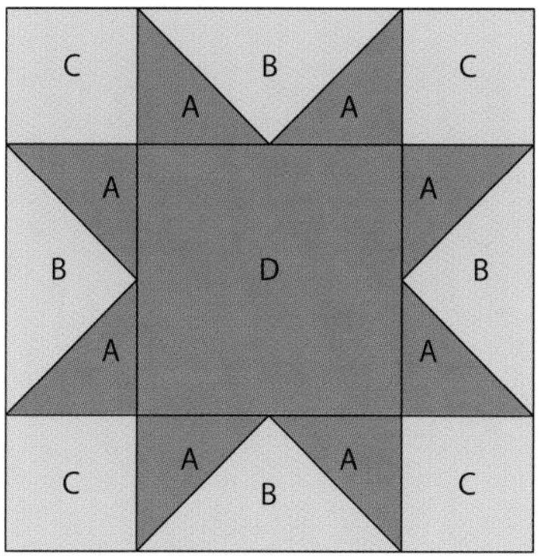

Sawtooth Star block

For each Sawtooth Star block, cut the following, and keep the materials for each block together. You will need to cut 13 blocks.

- Cut 8 blue squares 1½″ × 1½″ for piece A.
- Cut 4 light rectangles 1½″ × 2½″ for piece B.
- Cut 4 light squares 1½″ × 1½″ for piece C.
- Cut 1 blue square 2½″ × 2½″ for piece D.

Alternate blocks

- Cut 2 strips 4½″ × width of fabric.

  Subcut 12 squares 4½ × 4½″.

Half-square triangle border

From the blues:

- Cut 42 squares 2″ × 2″.

From the lights:

- Cut 42 squares 2″ × 2″.

Solid border

Wait to cut the borders until you have measured your quilt top. Measure the quilt center horizontally and vertically, and change the border measurements if necessary to fit your quilt.

- Cut 2 strips 4½″ × 22½″ for the side borders.
- Cut 2 strips 4½″ × 30½″ for the top and bottom borders.

Construction

Sawtooth Star Block

1. Refer to Making Flying Geese (page 13) for sewing instructions. Use matching A squares and B rectangles to make 4 Flying Geese units for each block.

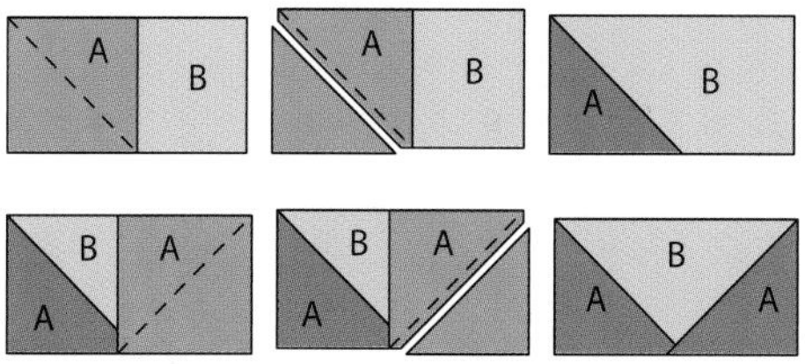

2. Sew a Flying Geese unit to 2 opposite sides of a D square. Press the seam allowance toward the D square.

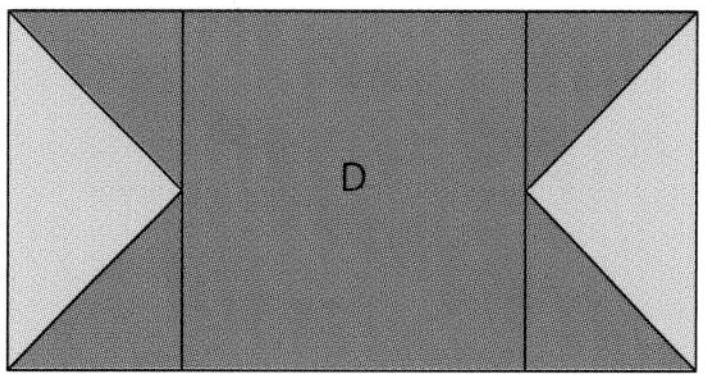

3. Sew a C square to each end of the 2 remaining Flying Geese units. Press the seam allowance toward the C squares.

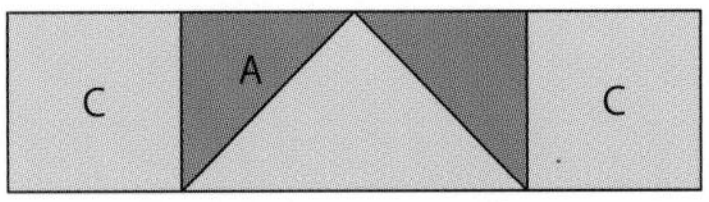

4. Sew a row from Step 3 to the 2 remaining sides of the unit from Step 2 to complete a block measuring 4½″ × 4½″.

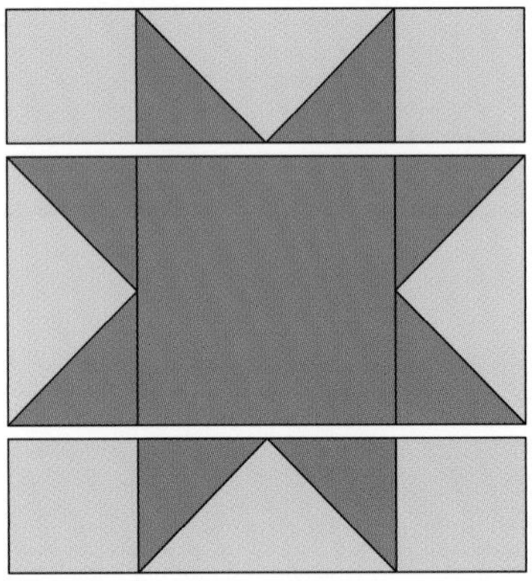

5. Repeat Steps 1–4 to make a total of 13 blocks.

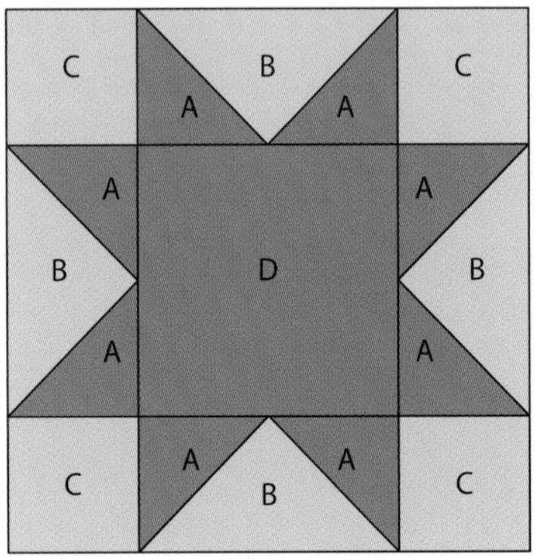

Sawtooth Star block. Make 13.

Half-Square Triangles

1. Refer to Making Half-Square Triangles (page 12). Pair a blue 2″ × 2″ square and a light 2″ × 2″ square to make 2 half-square triangles measuring 1½″ × 1½″.

2. Repeat Step 1 to make 84 half-square triangles total.

Quilt Assembly

1. Refer to the quilt assembly diagram (below) to arrange the 13 Sawtooth Stars and 12 alternate blocks in 5 rows of 5 blocks each. Starting with a Sawtooth Star in the upper right corner, alternate Sawtooth Stars and alternate blocks.

2. Sew the blocks in each row together, and then sew the rows together to complete the quilt center. Your top should measure 20½″ × 20½″ square.

3. Referring to the diagram for correct placement, sew together 20 half-square triangles for each side border. Attach the borders to each side of the quilt top.

4. Sew together 22 half-square triangles for the top and bottom border. Note the corner block placement.

5. Measure your top to check the size. If it is different than the pattern size, trim your border strips to fit.

6. Add a 4½″ × 22½″ border strip to the right and left side of the quilt top. Press the seam allowances toward the borders. Sew a 4½″ × 30½″ border strip to the top and bottom of the quilt to complete the top.

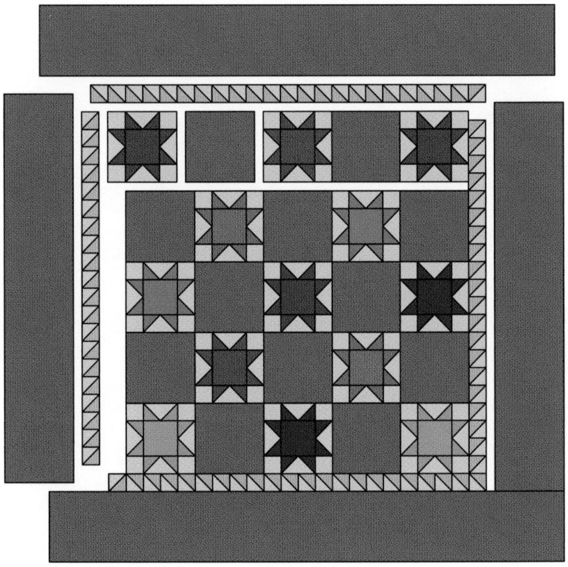

Quilt assembly

Finishing

Quilt using a favorite quilt design. This one is machine quilted using a grid design. Follow Finishing Your Quilt (page 14) to bind your quilt, and enjoy.

Mid-Century Projects: 1840–1870

Mid-century quilts were being made with fabrics created in both America and Europe. Natural dyes, such as madder and indigo, were still the popular choice during this time. Some of the colors would fade over time; greens and purples, for example, faded to brown. As more fabrics were produced in American mills, fabric patterns were getting smaller and more complex. Red and green Baltimore Album appliqué quilts were popular, along with album or signature block quilts.

Stripes, printed plaids, and paisleys were popular fabric choices. Green, chrome yellow, cheddar orange, Turkey red, and brown were commonly used with blues.

Designed and made by Annette Plog, quilted by Sheri Mecom

Steps to the Altar

Finished quilt: 63″ × 78″ • **Finished block:** 12″ × 12″

This quilt is made with a version of the Jacob's Ladder block. Scrappy blues, browns, golds, and lights are used to form the path, and the sashing and borders are made with an indigo print. The simple blocks create a bold grid pattern that can lend a modern touch.

Materials

Lights and darks: 3⁄8 yard each of 10 lights and 10 darks

Sashing and cornerstones: 13⁄8 yards

Border: 7⁄8 yard

Binding: 1⁄2 yard

Backing: 5 yards

Batting: 71″ × 86″

Cutting

Steps to the Altar blocks

Steps to the Altar block

You can make 2 blocks from 1 light and 1 dark color combination. These block cutting instructions will make 2 blocks.

From *each* of the 10 dark fabrics:

- Cut 2 strips 31⁄2″ × width of fabric.

  Subcut 16 squares 31⁄2″ × 31⁄2″ and 8 squares 21⁄2″ × 21⁄2″.

- Cut 1 strip 2″ × width of fabric.

  Subcut 16 squares 2″ × 2″.

From *each* of the 10 light fabrics:

- Cut 2 strips 31⁄2″ × width of fabric.

  Subcut 8 rectangles 31⁄2″ × 61⁄2″ and 10 squares 21⁄2″ × 21⁄2″.

- Cut 1 strip 2″ × width of fabric.

  Subcut 16 squares 2″ × 2″.

Sashing

- Cut 11 strips 31⁄2″ × width of fabric.

  Subcut 31 rectangles 31⁄2″ × 121⁄2″.

Cornerstones

- Cut 2 strips 2″ × width of fabric.

  Subcut 24 squares 2″ × 2″.

- Cut 24 squares 2″ × 2″ from any remaining light strips.

Border

- Cut 7 strips 31⁄2″ × width of fabric.

Construction

The Steps to the Altar block is made by combining a nine-patch unit, a four-patch unit, and a Flying Geese unit.

Nine-Patch Unit

Use the same light and dark fabric to make each unit.

1. Sew a light 2½″ × 2½″ square to 2 opposite sides of a dark 2½″ × 2½″ square. Make 2.

2. Sew a dark 2½″ × 2½″ square to 2 opposite sides of a light 2½″ × 2½″ square.

3. Sew the units from Step 1 to the top and bottom of the row from Step 2 to complete a block measuring 6½″ × 6½″. Press all seam allowances toward the darker fabric.

4. Repeat Steps 1–3 to make 20 units total, 1 for each Steps to the Altar block. You should have 2 blocks in each color combination.

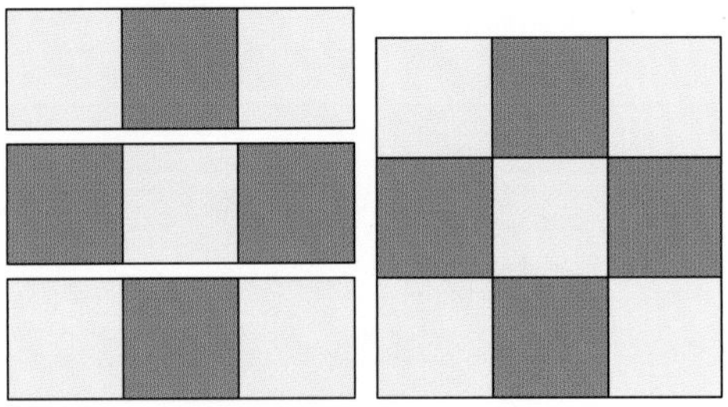

Nine-patch unit. Make 20.

Four-Patch Unit

Use the same light and dark fabric to make each unit.

1. Sew together a pair of light and dark 2″ × 2″ squares. Press the seam allowances toward the darker fabric. Make 2 pairs. Sew the pairs together to complete a four-patch measuring 3½″ × 3½″.

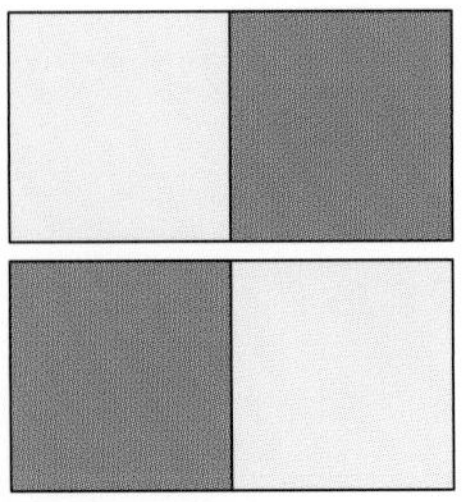

2. Using the same matching fabrics, repeat Step 1 to make a total of 8 units. You will use 4 for each block, so 1 color combination makes enough four-patches for 2 blocks.

3. Repeat Steps 1 and 2 to make a total of 100 units.

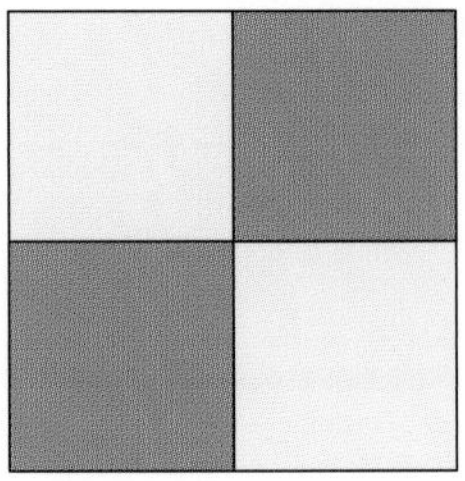

Four-patch unit. Make 100, 4 for each block.

Flying Geese Unit

Refer to Making Flying Geese (page 13) for sewing instructions. Use matching 3½″ × 3½″ squares and 3½″ × 6½″ rectangles to make 8 Flying Geese units from each color combination. You will use 4 for each block, 100 total.

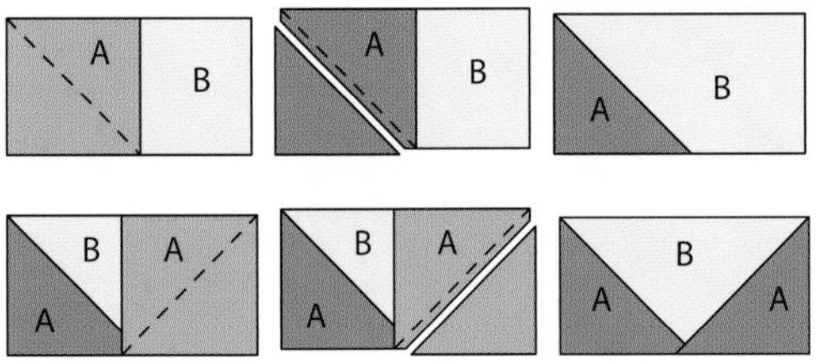

Flying Geese unit. Make 100, 4 for each block.

Block Assembly

1. Referring to the block assembly diagram (below) and using block units from matching fabrics, arrange a nine-patch unit in the center, with a Flying Geese unit on each side and a four-patch unit in each corner. Sew the units together in rows, and then sew the rows together to complete a block measuring 12½″ × 12½″.

2. Repeat Step 1 to make a total of 20 blocks, 2 from each color combination.

Steps to the Altar block. Make 20.

Sashing Cornerstones

Repeat Four-Patch Unit, Steps 1 and 2 (previous page) with 2″ × 2″ sashing squares and 24 light 2″ × 2″ squares to make 12 cornerstone units.

Quilt Assembly

1. Referring to the quilt assembly diagram (page 42), arrange the blocks in 5 rows of 4 blocks each. Place a vertical sashing rectangle between each block. Between the rows, arrange the horizontal sashing rectangles and cornerstones.

2. Sew the units in each row together, and then sew the rows together to complete the quilt center. It should measure 57½″ × 72½″.

3. Measure your top to check the size. If it is different than the pattern size, trim your border strips to fit during the next step.

4. Sew the border strips together end to end. Subcut 2 strips 72½″ and 2 strips 63½″. Sew a 72½″ strip to each side of the quilt top. Sew the 63½″ strips to the top and the bottom of the quilt to complete the top.

Quilt assembly

Finishing

Quilt using a favorite quilt design. This one is machine quilted using an overall fan design.

Follow Finishing Your Quilt (page 14) to bind your quilt, and enjoy.

Designed and made by Annette Plog, quilted by Kerry Coburn

Vicksburg Stars

Finished quilt: 61″ × 81½″ • **Finished block:** 6″ × 6″

Who doesn't love the Sawtooth Star block? These scrappy stars are arranged in rows and sashed with an indigo stripe. The stars are both light and dark with the opposite background color. Remember to use some white fabrics as lights to make your stars twinkle!

Materials

Lights: 8 fat eighths

Mediums: 8 fat eighths

Darks: 8 fat eighths

Setting triangles: 1½ yards

Sashing: 2 yards

Border: 2 yards

Binding: ½ yard

Backing: 5 yards

Batting: 69″ × 89″

Cutting

Sawtooth Star blocks

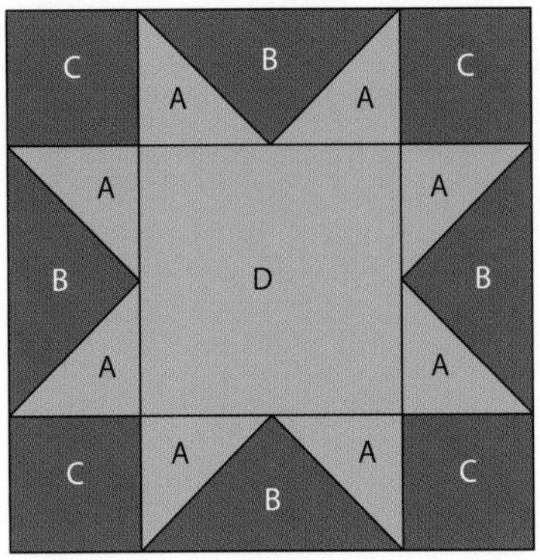

Sawtooth Star block

For each Sawtooth Star block, cut the following, and keep the materials for each block together. You will need to cut 32 blocks. Make half of the blocks with dark stars and half with light stars. You may use mediums as dark or light, depending on the fabric with which they are paired.

Cut each block from 2 contrasting fabrics.

From the first fabric:

- Cut 8 squares 2″ × 2″ for piece A.
- Cut 1 square 3½″ × 3½″ for piece D.

From contrasting fabric:

- Cut 4 rectangles 2″ × 3½″ for piece B.
- Cut 4 squares 2″ × 2″ for piece C.

Setting triangles

- Cut 14 squares 9¾″ × 9¾″. Cut each square in quarters diagonally to yield 56 side setting triangles.
- Cut 8 squares 5¼″ × 5¼″. Cut each square in half diagonally to yield 16 corner setting triangles.

Sashing

You may want to cut your strips a little longer in case your quilt turns out to be a slightly different size than the pattern size. You can trim the strips after you have assembled the columns of stars.

- On the *length* of the fabric, cut 3 strips 5″ × 68½″.

Tip

Cutting Sashing Strips with Border Print Fabric

If you find a great columnar print for sashing, you may want to fussy cut the sashing strips to highlight the design in your fabric. If you fussy cut the sashing, the width will depend on the design in the fabric. If your sashing width is different than 5″, remember to adjust the top and bottom border sizes to match the finished width of the quilt center.

Border

Wait to cut the borders until you have measured your quilt top. Measure the quilt center horizontally and vertically, and change the border measurements if necessary to fit your quilt.

On the *length* of the fabric:

- Cut 2 strips 7¼″ × 68½″ for the side borders.
- Cut 2 strips 7¼″ × 61½″ for the top and bottom borders.

NOTE If you have changed the size of the sash width, remember to change the length of your top and bottom borders to match your quilt width.

Construction

Sawtooth Star Block

1. Refer to Making Flying Geese (page 13) for sewing instructions. Use matching A squares and matching B rectangles to make 4 Flying Geese units for each Sawtooth Star block.

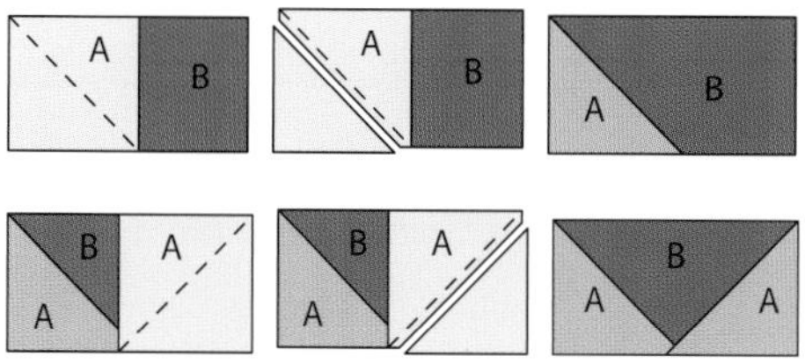

2. Sew a Flying Geese unit to 2 opposite sides of a matching D square. Press the seam allowance toward the D square.

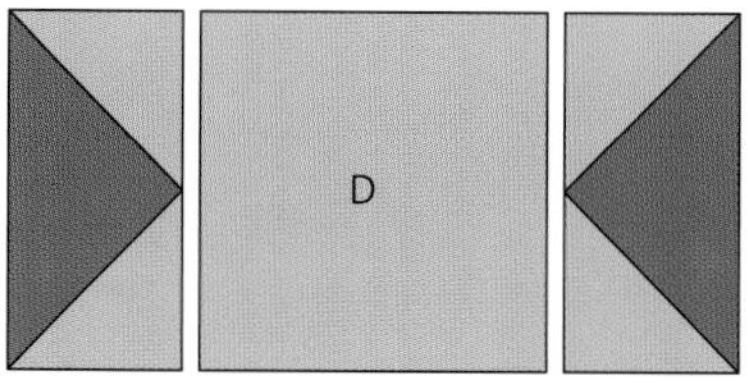

3. Sew a matching C square to each end of the 2 remaining Flying Geese units. Press the seam allowance toward the C squares.

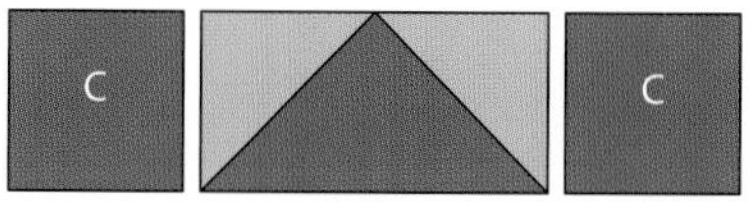

4. Sew a row from Step 3 to the 2 remaining sides of the unit from Step 2 to complete a block measuring 6½″ × 6½″.

5. Repeat Steps 1–4 to make a total of 32 blocks.

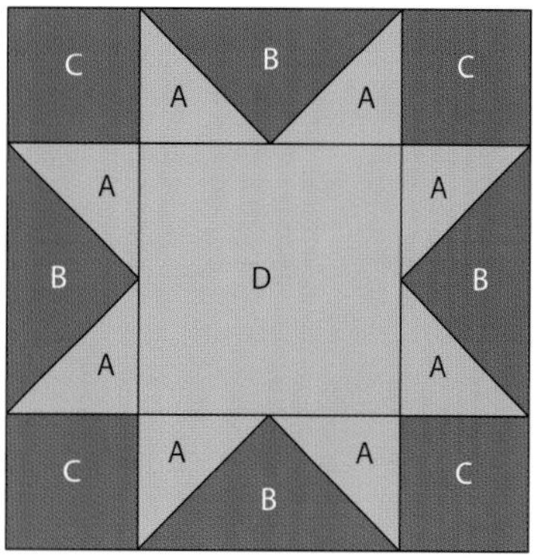

Sawtooth Star block. Make 32.

Star Columns

1. Sew a side setting triangle to the left side of a Sawtooth Star block and a corner setting triangle to the opposite side of the block. Press the seam allowances toward the setting triangles. Add a corner setting triangle to the top left side of the unit to complete the top star for each column. Make 4.

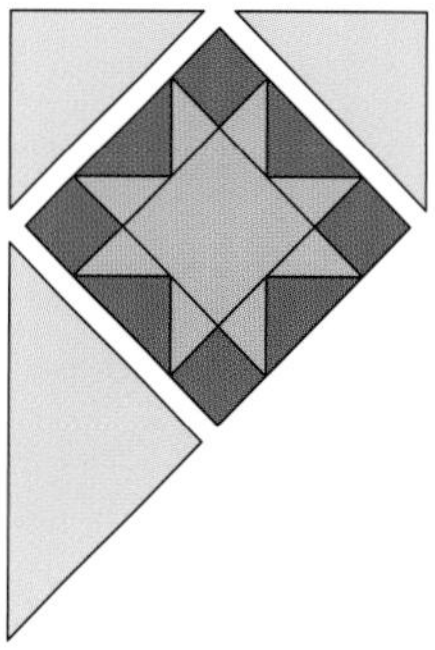

2. Sew a side setting triangle to 2 opposite sides of a Sawtooth Star block. Press the seam allowances toward the setting triangles. Make 24 blocks, 6 for each column.

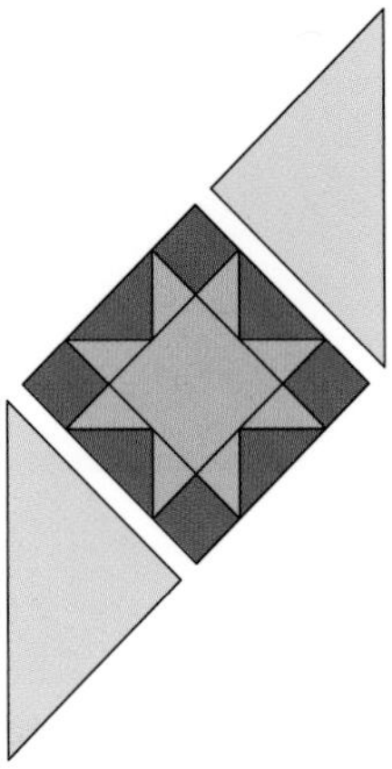

3. Sew a side setting triangle to the right side of a Sawtooth Star block and a corner setting triangle to the opposite side of the block. Press the seam allowances toward the setting triangles. Add a corner setting triangle to the bottom right side of the unit to complete the bottom star for each column. Make 4.

4. Sew together 4 star columns. The columns should measure 68½″ in length.

Quilt Assembly

1. Measure the length of the star columns and trim your sashings to match the columns.

2. Sew a sashing strip between each set of columns to create the quilt center. The quilt center should measure 48″ × 68½″.

3. Trim the side borders to the same length as the sashing strips and attach one to each side of the quilt.

4. Check the width of the quilt center, including the side borders, and trim your top and bottom border lengths to match. Sew a border to the top and bottom of the quilt.

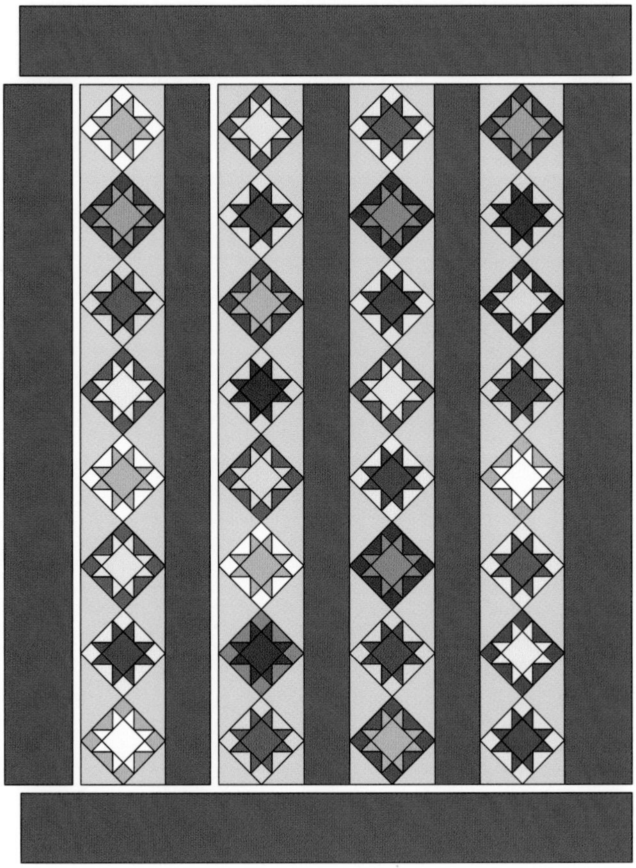

Quilt assembly

Finishing

Quilt using a favorite quilt design. This one is machine quilted using an overall fan design. Follow Finishing Your Quilt (page 14) to bind your quilt, and enjoy.

Designed, made, and quilted by Sheri Mecom

Sawtooth Squares

Finished quilt: 72½" × 86¾" • **Finished block:** 10" × 10"

Sawtooth Squares was inspired by an antique quilt I saw at a quilt show. I love the scrappy blue blocks, and the large alternate blocks are the perfect place to show off some beautiful quilting. The Sawtooth inner border works well with the blocks, and the striped blue border finishes the quilt perfectly.

Materials

Blues and indigos: ⅜ yard each of 10 blues

Tan: 3½ yards

Border: 2¼ yards

Backing: 5½ yards

Binding: ⅝ yard

Batting: 80″ × 95″

Cutting

Sawtooth Square blocks

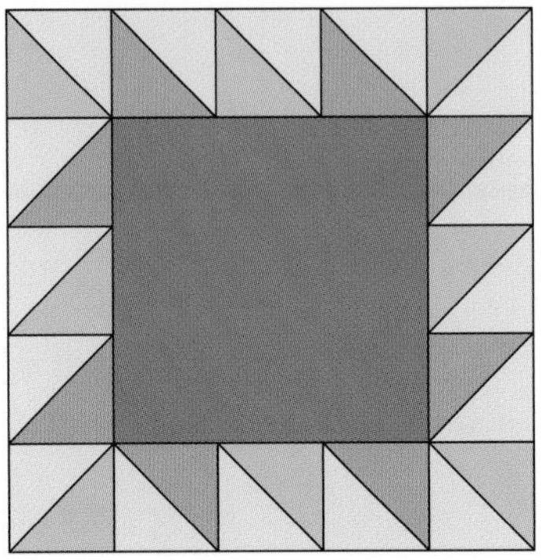

Sawtooth Square block

From *each* blue (enough for 2 blocks):

- Cut 2 squares 6½″ × 6½″ for the block centers.
- Cut 16 squares 3″ × 3″ for the half-square triangles.

From the tan:

- Cut 160 squares 3″ × 3″.

Alternate blocks and setting triangles

From the tan:

- Cut 4 squares 15½″ × 15½″ for the side setting triangles. Cut each square in quarters diagonally to yield 4 side setting triangles, 16 total. You will have 2 extra.
- Cut 12 squares 10½″ × 10½″ for the alternate blocks.
- Cut 2 squares 8″ × 8″ for the corner setting triangles. Cut each square in half diagonally to yield 2 triangles, 4 total.

Sawtooth border

From the blues:

- Cut 65 squares 3″ × 3″.

From the tans:

- Cut 65 squares 3″ × 3″.

Solid border

You may want to wait to cut the borders until you have measured your quilt top. Measure the quilt center horizontally and vertically, and change the border measurements if necessary to fit your quilt.

On the *length* of the fabric:

- Cut 2 strips 6½″ × 75¼″ for the side borders.
- Cut 2 strips 6½″ × 73″ for the top and bottom borders.

Construction

Sawtooth Square Block

1. Refer to Making Half-Square Triangles (page 12) for sewing instructions. Use a pair of blue and tan 3″ × 3″ squares to make 2 half-square triangles measuring 2½″ × 2½″.

2. Repeat Step 1 to make 16 half-square triangles for each block, 320 total.

3. Referring to the block assembly diagram, place 16 half-square triangles around a blue center square, arranging the colors in a pleasing manner. From 2 opposite sides of the center square, sew together a set of 3 half-square triangles. Sew the triangle units to the center.

4. From the remaining sides of the block, sew together the sets of 5 half-square triangles. Sew the triangle units to the remaining sides of the block to complete a block measuring 10½″ × 10½″.

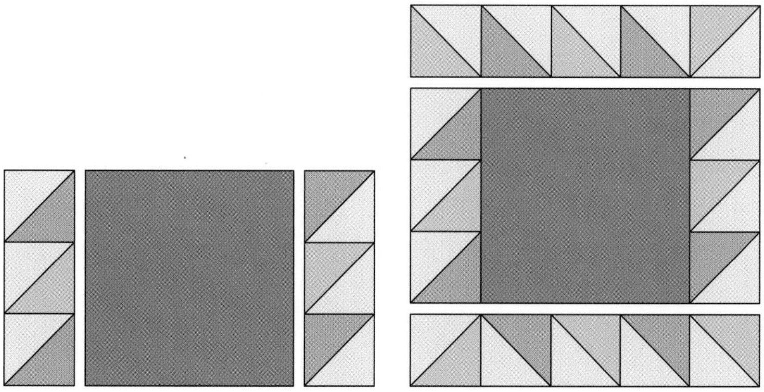

Block assembly

5. Repeat Steps 3 and 4 to make a total of 20 Sawtooth Square blocks.

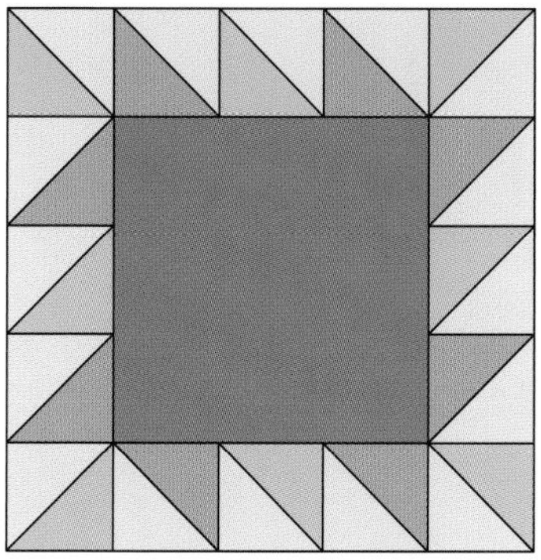

Sawtooth Square block. Make 20.

Half-Square Triangle Borders

1. Pair up 65 blue and tan 3″ × 3″squares to make 130 half-square triangles measuring 2½″ × 2½″.

2. Referring to the quilt assembly diagram (page 50) for the correct placement of the half-square triangles, piece together 2 sets of 35 half-square triangles for the side borders. Piece together 2 sets of 30 half-square triangles for the top and bottom borders.

Quilt Assembly

1. Referring to the quilt assembly diagram (page 50), arrange the Sawtooth Square blocks on point in 5 rows of 4 blocks each. Fill in between the blocks with the 12 alternate squares. Place the side setting triangles and corner setting triangles around the outer edge of the quilt.

2. Sew the quilt center blocks together in diagonal rows, starting at the top left corner. Sew the rows together to complete the quilt center. Your top should measure 57″ × 71¼″.

3. Sew a set of 35 half-square triangles to each side of the quilt top.

4. Sew a set of 30 half-square triangles to the top and bottom of the quilt top.

5. Measure your top to check the size. If it is different than the pattern size, trim your border strips to fit.

6. Sew a 6½″ × 75¼″ border strip to each side of the quilt top. Press the seam allowances toward the borders. Sew a 6½″ × 73″ border strip to the top and bottom of the quilt to complete the top.

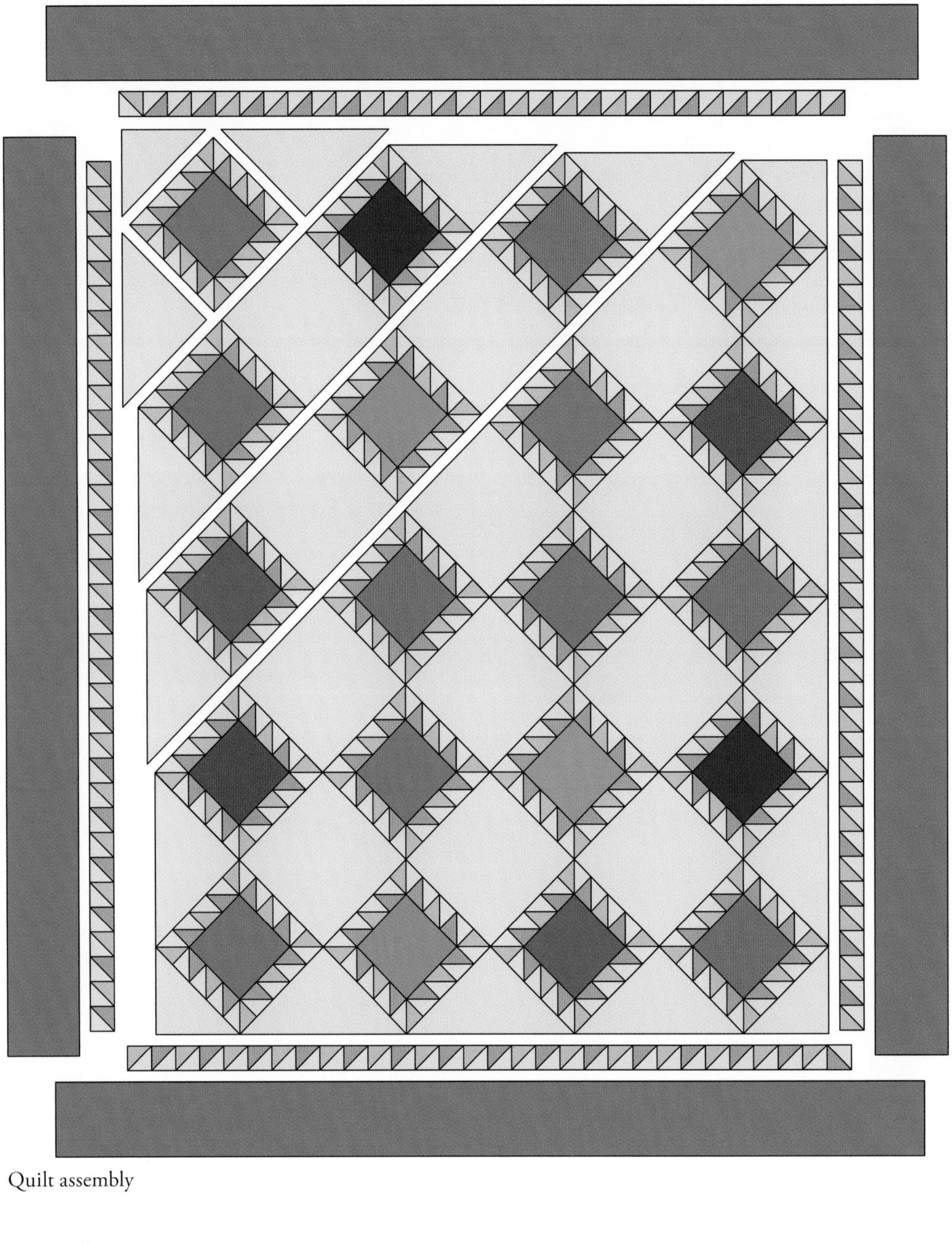

Quilt assembly

Finishing

Quilt using a favorite quilt design. This one is machine quilted using a grid design in the squares and a beautiful feathered wreath in the alternate blocks. Follow Finishing Your Quilt (page 14) to bind your quilt, and enjoy.

Designed and made by Annette Plog, quilted by Kerry Coburn

French Blue Flower Pots

Finished quilt: 42″ × 52½″ • **Finished block:** 6″ × 6″

This quilt makes me think of the southern French countryside. The flower pot blues are soft yet strong, surrounded by a blue ombré stripe and a small blue floral border. This quilt is just the right size for a crib quilt or lap throw.

Materials

Blues: ¼ yard each of 5 blues for flower pots

Lights: ¼ yard each of 5 lights for flower pots

Sashing: ½ yard

Cornerstones and half-cornerstones: ⅜ yard

Setting triangles: ½ yard

Inner border: ¼ yard

Outer border: ¾ yard

Backing: 3 yards

Binding: ½ yard

Batting: 50″ × 60″

Cutting

Flower Pot blocks

Flower Pot block

Each blue fabric will yield 4 blocks. You will have 2 blocks left over.

From *each* blue:

- Cut 4 squares 2″ × 2″ for piece A.
- Cut 4 rectangles 2″ × 3½″ for piece B.
- Cut 12 squares 2½″ × 2½″ for piece C.

From *each* light fabric:

- Cut 12 squares 2½″ × 2½″ for piece C.
- Cut 12 squares 2″ × 2″ for piece D.
- Cut 8 rectangles 2″ × 3½″ for piece E.

Sashing

- Cut 8 strips 2″ × width of fabric.

  From each strip, subcut 6 rectangles 2″ × 6½″, 48 total.

Cornerstones and half-cornerstones

- Cut 1 strip 2″ × width of fabric.

  Subcut 17 squares 2″ × 2″ for cornerstones.

- Cut 1 strip 4⅛″ × width of fabric.

  Subcut 4 squares 4⅛″ × 4⅛″.

  Subcut each square in quarters diagonally to yield 4 half-cornerstone triangles, 16 total. You will need 14.

Setting triangles

- Cut 3 squares 9¾″ × 9¾″. Cut each square in quarters diagonally to yield 4 side setting triangles, 12 total. You will need 10.
- Cut 2 squares 5⅛″ × 5⅛″ for corner setting triangles. Cut each square in half diagonally to yield 2 triangles, 4 total.

Inner border

You may want to wait to trim the borders until you have measured your quilt top. Measure the quilt center horizontally and vertically, and change the border measurements if necessary to fit your quilt.

- Cut 4 strips 1½″ × width of fabric.

Outer border

- Cut 5 strips 4½″ × width of fabric.

Construction

Flower Pot Block

Each blue and light fabric combination will yield 4 Flower Pot blocks. Use matching fabrics for each block.

1. Refer to Making Half-Square Triangles (page 12) for sewing instructions. Using matching fabrics, pair 12 blue and 12 light 2½″ × 2½″ squares to make 24 half-square triangles measuring 2″ × 2″. This will be enough units for 4 blocks.

2. Referring to the block assembly diagram, arrange 6 half-square triangles (C), 1 A square, 1 B rectangle, 3 D squares, and 2 E rectangles.

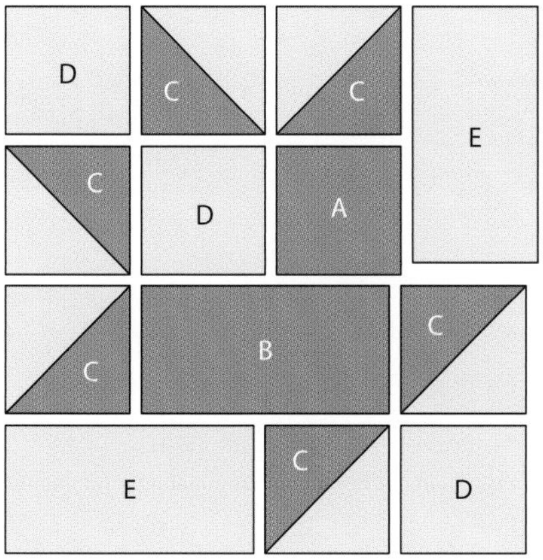

Block assembly

3. Sew a D square to 2 half-square triangles (C). Press the seam allowances to the left.

4. Sew a half-square triangle (C) to a D square and an A square. Press the seam allowances to the right.

5. Sew the 2 units together and press the seam down toward the C/D/A unit. Sew an E rectangle to the right side of the unit. Press the seam allowances toward D.

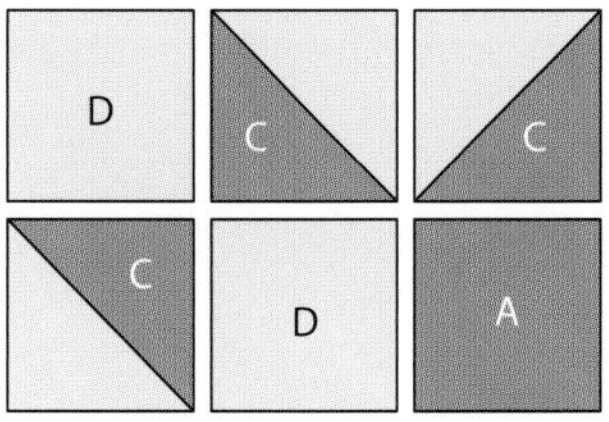

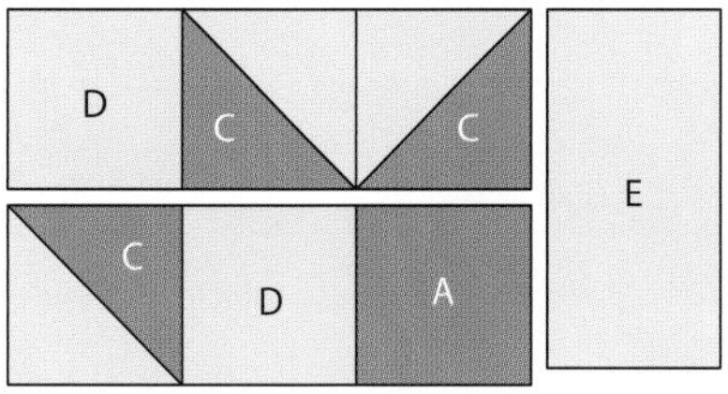

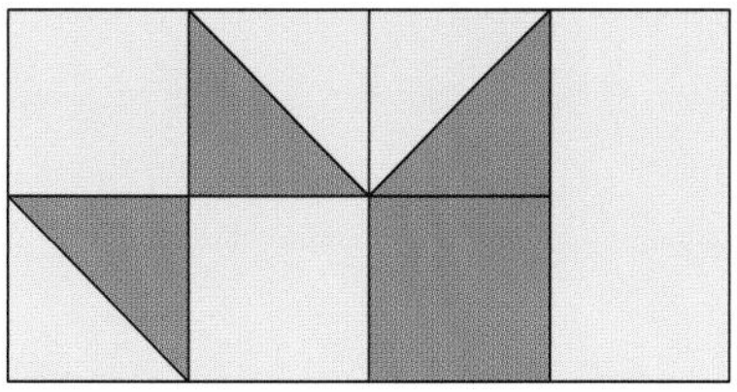

6. Sew a half-square triangle (C) to each end of a B rectangle. Press the seam allowances to the left.

7. Sew an E rectangle to a half-square triangle (C) and a D square. Press the seam allowances toward the right.

8. Sew the 2 units together and press the seam down toward the E/C/D unit.

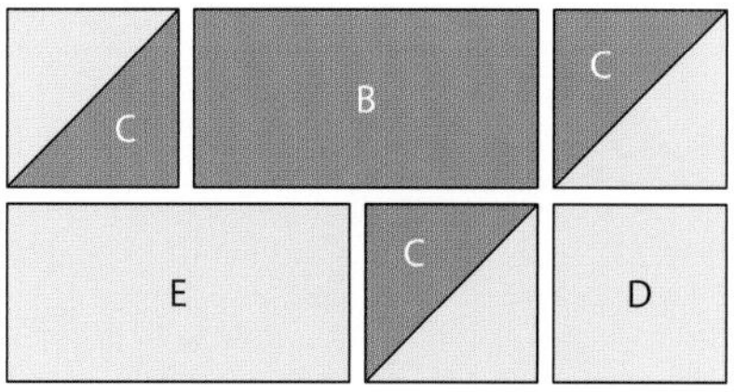

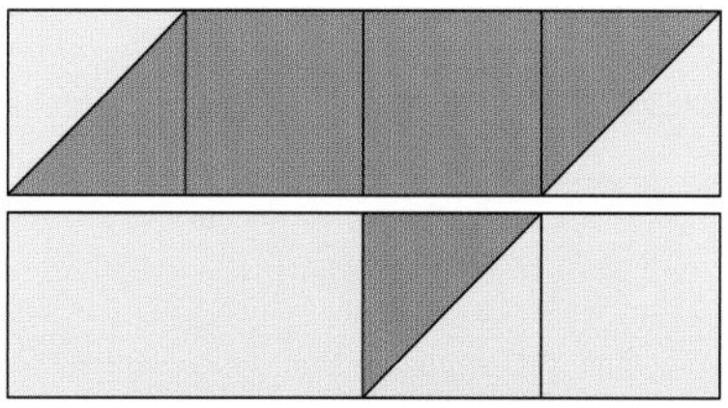

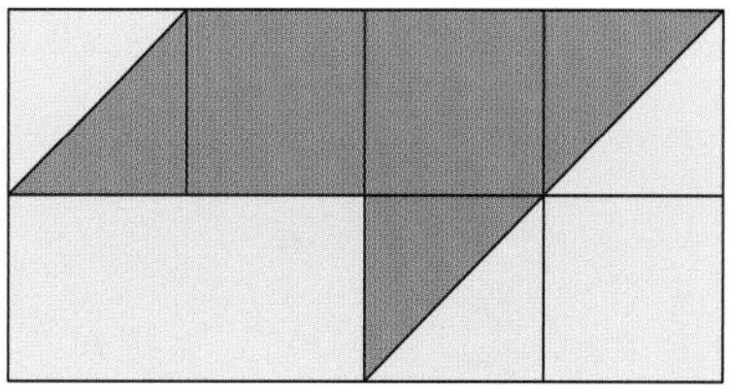

9. Sew the unit from Step 5 to the top of the unit from Step 8 to complete a block measuring 6½″ × 6½″. Press the seam allowance toward the bottom unit.

10. Repeat Steps 2–9 to make 3 more blocks from this blue and light combination.

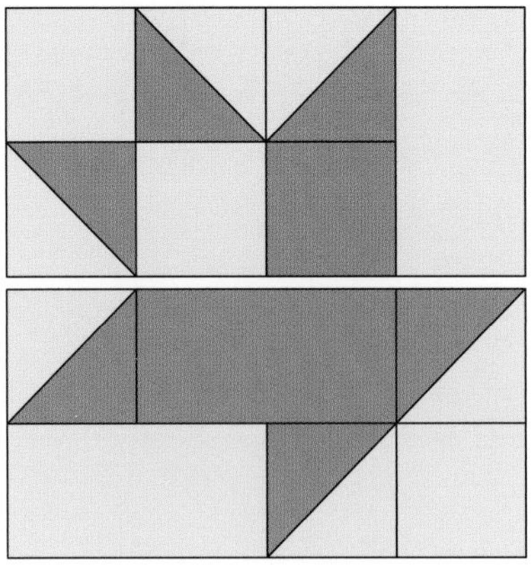

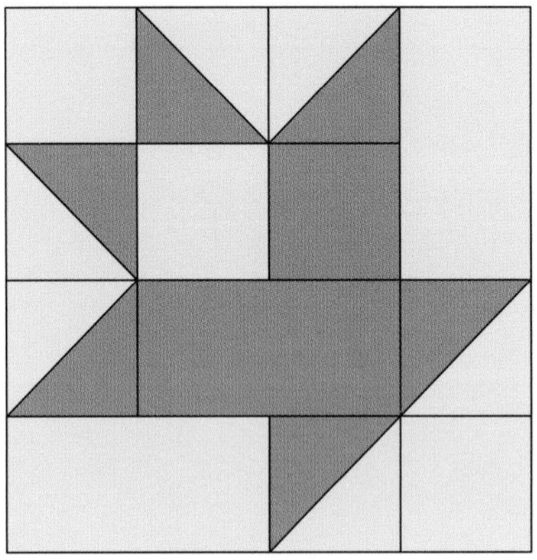

11. Repeat Steps 2–10 with the other pairs of blues and lights to make a total of 20 blocks. You will only need 18 blocks for the quilt. The extra blocks will give you flexibility in block placement.

Quilt Assembly

1. Referring to the quilt assembly diagram (next page), arrange the Flower Pot blocks on point in 4 rows of 3 blocks each. Fill the spaces between the blocks with the 6 remaining Flower Pot blocks.

2. Place sashing strips on each side of each block, with cornerstones between the sashing and half-cornerstones at the outer edges of the quilt. Fill in the outer edge with side setting triangles and corner setting triangles.

3. Sew the quilt together in diagonal rows. Starting with the sashing row at the top left corner, sew all the sashing rows together first.

4. Sew the blocks in each row together, with sashing in between each block and the setting triangles at the ends of the rows.

5. Sew the rows together to complete the quilt center. It should measure 32½″ × 43″.

6. Measure your top to check the size. If it is different than the pattern size, trim your border strips to fit during the next 2 steps.

7. Sew the inner border strips together in pairs to make long strips. Cut a 43″ side border and a 34½″ top or bottom border from each pieced strip. Sew a 43″ border to each side of the quilt. Sew the 34½″ strips to the top and bottom of the quilt. It should measure 34½″ × 45½″.

8. Sew the outer border strips together end to end to make a long strip. Cut 2 strips 45″ and 2 strips 42½″. Sew a 45″ strip to each side of the quilt. Sew the 42½″ strips to the top and bottom of the quilt to complete the top.

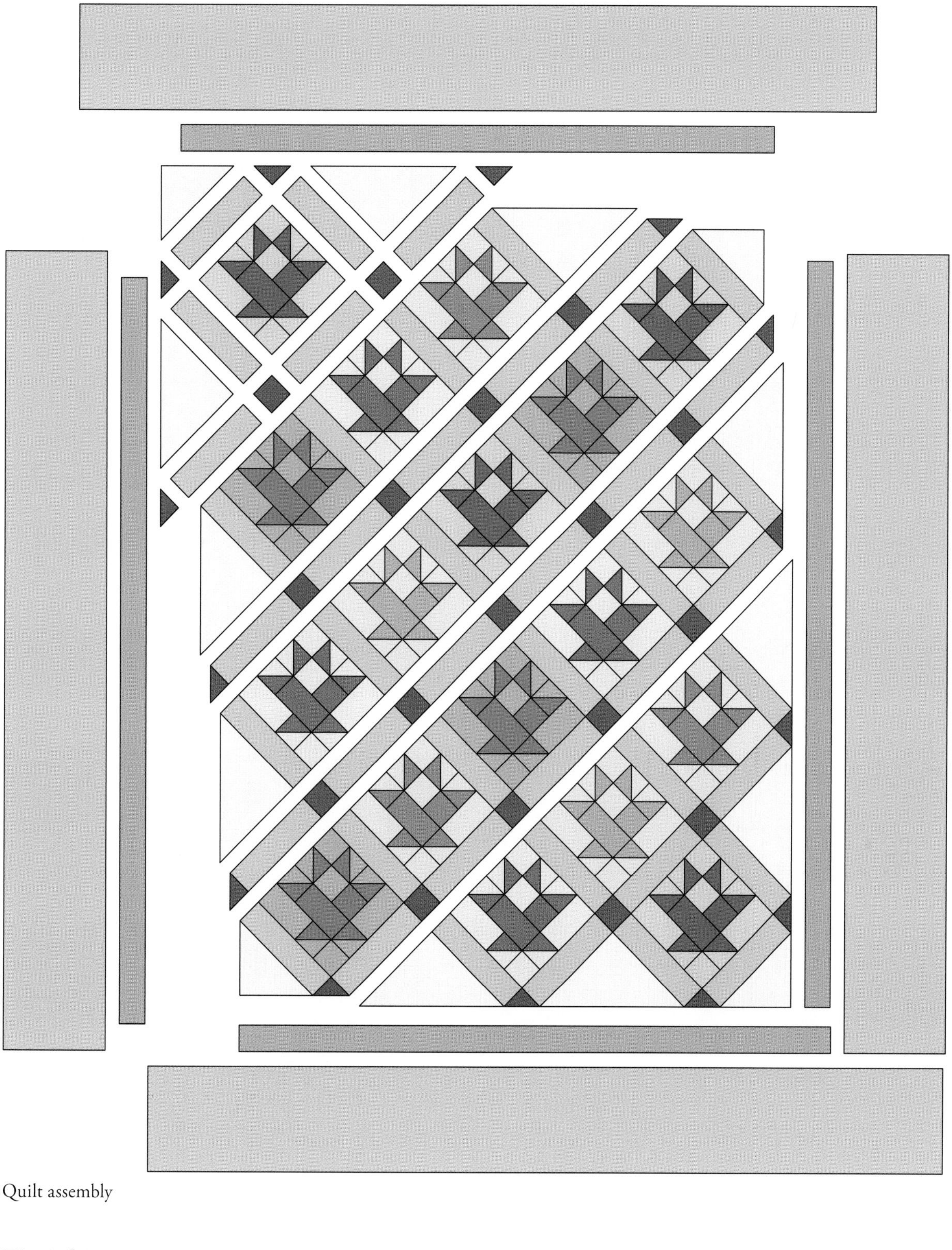

Quilt assembly

Finishing

Quilt using a favorite quilt design. This one is machine quilted using an allover floral design. Follow Finishing Your Quilt (page 14) to bind your quilt, and enjoy.

Designed, made, and quilted by Annette Plog

PETITE PINWHEELS

Finished quilt: 16″ × 26″ • **Finished block:** 2″ × 2″

Petite Pinwheels is the smallest of the quilt projects. This Pinwheel block measures 2″ square! This quilt also lets the quilter use a wonderful double-pink fabric, a mid-century favorite that features a pink ground with a small pink print. Indigo and double pink was a common pairing and is still one of today's favorites.

Materials

Indigos: 1 fat eighth of 4 or more indigos

Pink: ¼ yard

Light: ¼ yard

Sashing, border, and binding: ½ yard

Backing: ¾ yard

Batting: 20″ × 30″

Cutting

Pinwheel blocks

Pinwheel block

From the light:

- Cut 60 squares 2″ × 2″.

From *each* indigo:

- Cut 15 squares 2″ × 2″.

Alternate square

From the pink:

- Cut 30 squares 2½″ × 2½″.

Sashing

- Cut 6 strips 1½″ × 12½″.

Side border

- Cut 2 strips 2½″ × 26½″.

Construction

Pinwheel Block

1. Refer to Making Half-Square Triangles (page 12) for sewing instructions. Pair the light and dark 2″ × 2″ squares to make 120 half-square triangles measuring 1½″ × 1½″.

2. Place 4 half-square triangles in a pinwheel formation.

3. Sew the top 2 half-square triangles together and then the bottom 2 half-square triangles together. Sew the top unit to the bottom unit to complete a block measuring 2½″ × 2½″.

Block assembly

4. Repeat Steps 2 and 3 to make 30 Pinwheel blocks.

Pinwheel block

Quilt Assembly

1. Referring to the quilt assembly diagram (at right), arrange 6 Pinwheel blocks and 6 pink squares in 2 rows of 6 blocks each. Alternate the Pinwheel blocks and pink squares, starting with a Pinwheel block in the upper right corner. Sew the blocks in each row together, and then sew the rows together to make a section measuring 12½″ × 4½″. Make 5 pinwheel sections.

2. Sew a 1½″ × 12½″ sashing strip to the bottom of each pinwheel section. Press toward the sashing.

3. Sew the sections from Step 2 together; then sew the last sashing strip to the top of the quilt top. Your top should measure 12½″ × 26½″.

4. Measure your top to check the size. If it is different than the pattern size, trim your border strips to fit during the next step.

5. Sew a 2½″ × 26½″ border strip to each side of the quilt to complete the top.

Quilt assembly

Finishing

Quilt using a favorite quilt design. This one is machine quilted using a grid design. Follow Finishing Your Quilt (page 14) to bind your quilt, and enjoy.

Late-Century Projects: 1870–1900

The late decades of the nineteenth century in America saw the development and more common use of synthetic dyes. These dyes were more reliable and colorfast, so colors such as purple and black could be used without much fear of bleeding or fading.

America's centennial celebration sparked the popularity of patriotic prints, such as stars, stripes, and conversational prints. With the death of Prince Albert of England, darker colors, such as blacks, indigos, grays, and dark purples featuring small prints became popular in America and were used in clothing and in quilts. Shirtings with small geometric motifs, stripes, and figures were popular, along with the small red, yellow, and cheddar calico-style prints.

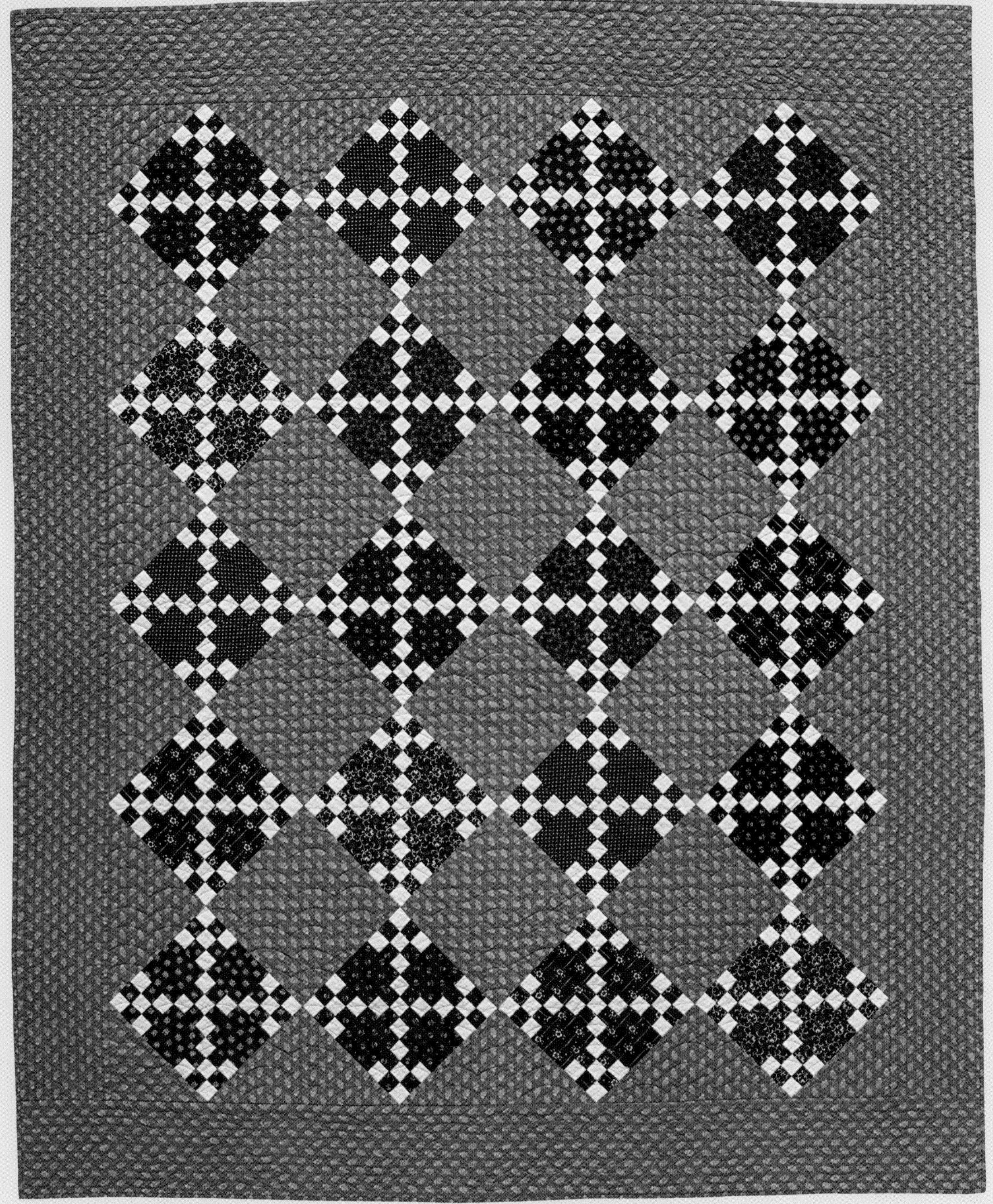

Designed and made by Annette Plog, quilted by Sheri Mecom

Prairie Sky Nine-Patch

Finished quilt: 63″ × 75½″ • **Finished block:** 9″ × 9″

The Nine-Patch block is a popular and versatile quilt pattern. This project was inspired by an 1870s antique quilt. The Double Nine-Patch block uses different indigos and lights. The white fabric reminds me of the stars in the prairie sky. The alternate block and border is a wonderful green color.

Materials

Indigo: ½ yard each of 5 indigos

Cream: 1⅛ yards

Green: 1⅞ yards

Border and binding: 2 yards

Backing: 4¾ yards

Batting: 71″ × 83″

Cutting

Double Nine-Patch blocks

Double Nine-Patch block

Each indigo fabric will yield 4 blocks.

From *each* indigo:

- Cut 4 strips 1½″ × width of fabric for the Nine-Patch strip sets.
- Cut 2 strips 3½″ × width of fabric.

  Subcut 16 squares 3½″ × 3½″.

From the cream:

- Cut 25 strips 1½″ × width of fabric for the Nine-Patch strip sets.

Alternate blocks

From the green:

- Cut 3 strips 9½″ × width of fabric.

  Subcut 12 squares 9½″ × 9½″.

Setting triangles

From the green:

- Cut 2 strips 14″ × width of fabric.

  Subcut 4 squares 14″ × 14″. Cut each square in quarters diagonally to yield 16 side setting triangles. You will use only 14.

- Cut 2 squares 7¼″ × 7¼″. Cut each square in half diagonally to yield 4 corner setting triangles.

Border

You may want to cut your strips a little longer in case your quilt turns out to be a slightly different size from the pattern. Measure the quilt center horizontally and vertically, and change the border measurements if necessary to fit your quilt.

On the *length* of the fabric:

- Cut 2 strips 6½″ × 64″ for the side borders.
- Cut 2 strips 6½″ × 63½″ for the top and bottom borders.

Construction

Nine-Patch Block

1. Using 2 cream and 1 indigo 1½″ strips, make a 3½″ strip set with the indigo in the center. Press the seam allowances toward the darker fabric. Make 2 strip sets.

2. Cut the strip sets into 40 segments 1½″ × 3½″.

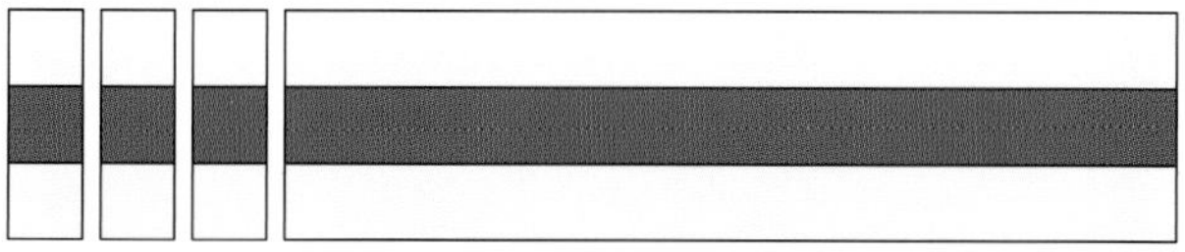

3. Using 1 cream and 2 indigo 1½″ strips from the same fabric you used in Step 1, make a strip set with the cream in the center. Press the seam allowances toward the darker fabric. Cut the strip sets into 20 segments 1½″ × 3½″.

4. Sew a segment from Step 2 to each side of a segment from Step 3 to make a Nine-Patch block measuring 3½″ × 3½″. Make 20.

5. Repeat Steps 1–4 to make 20 blocks from each indigo fabric, 100 blocks total. You will need 5 blocks for each Double Nine-Patch block.

Nine-Patch block

Double Nine-Patch Block

Use units in matching fabrics to make each block. You will be able to make 4 Double Nine-Patch blocks from each indigo fabric.

1. Sew a Nine-Patch block to 2 opposite sides of a blue 3½″ × 3½″ square. Make 2.

2. Sew a blue 3½″ × 3½″ square to each side of a Nine-Patch block.

3. Sew a unit from Step 1 to the top and bottom of the unit from Step 2 to complete a block measuring 9½″ × 9½″.

Double Nine-Patch block assembly

4. Repeat Steps 1–3 to make 20 blocks total.

Double Nine-Patch block. Make 20.

Quilt Assembly

1. Referring to the quilt assembly diagram (next page), arrange the blocks in diagonal rows, placing the various indigos in a pleasing manner. Add the alternate blocks, setting triangles, and corners.

2. Sew the quilt together in diagonal rows, starting at the top left corner. Sew the rows together to complete the top center. It should measure 51½″ × 64″.

3. Measure your top to check the size. If it is different than the pattern size, trim your border strips to fit.

4. Sew a 6½″ × 64″ border strip to each side of the quilt top. Press the seam allowance toward the border. Sew a 6½″ × 63½″ border strip to the top and bottom to complete the top.

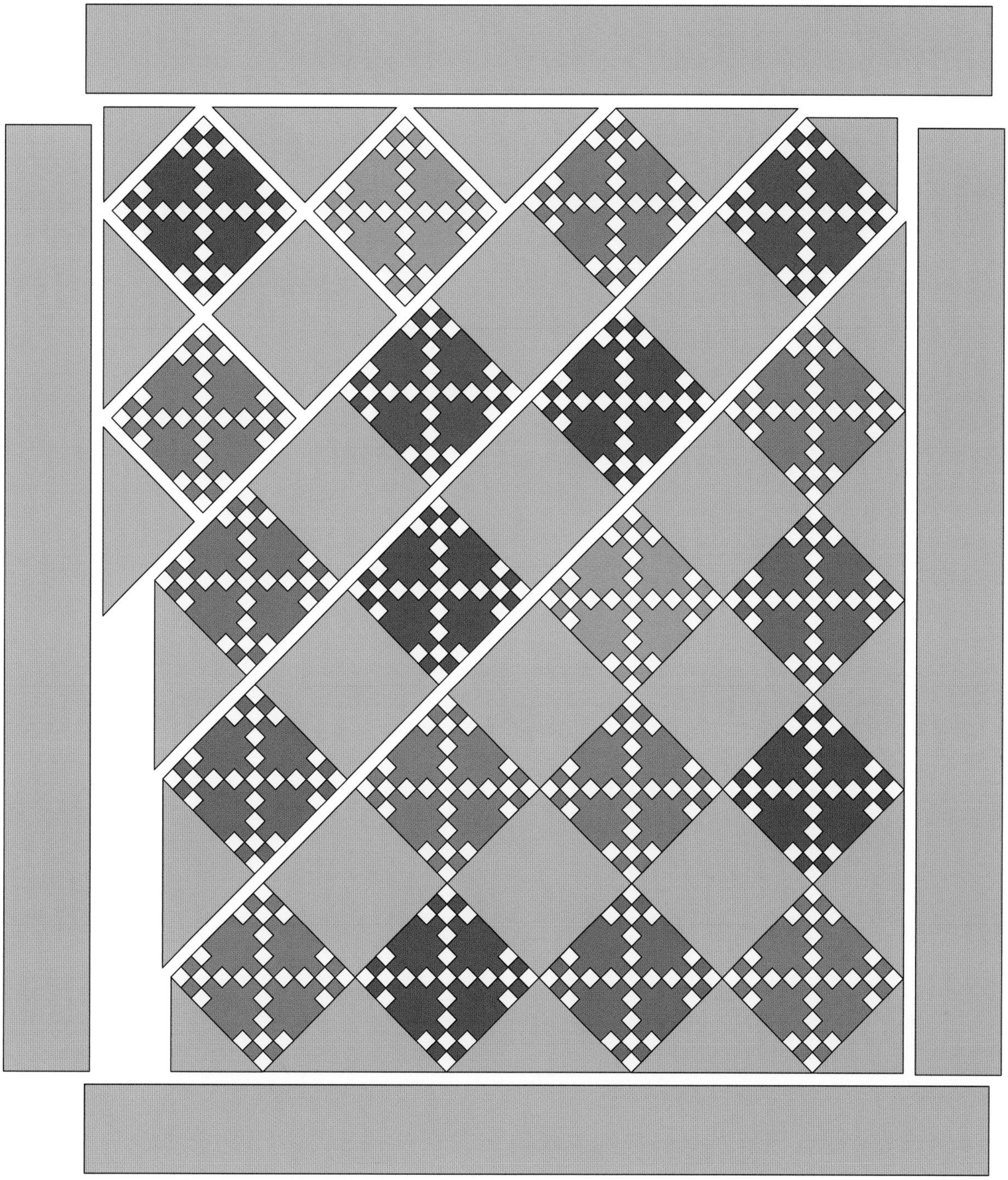
Quilt assembly

Finishing

Quilt using a favorite quilt design. This one is machine quilted using an overall wave design, with a cable in the border. Follow Finishing Your Quilt (page 14) to bind your quilt, and enjoy.

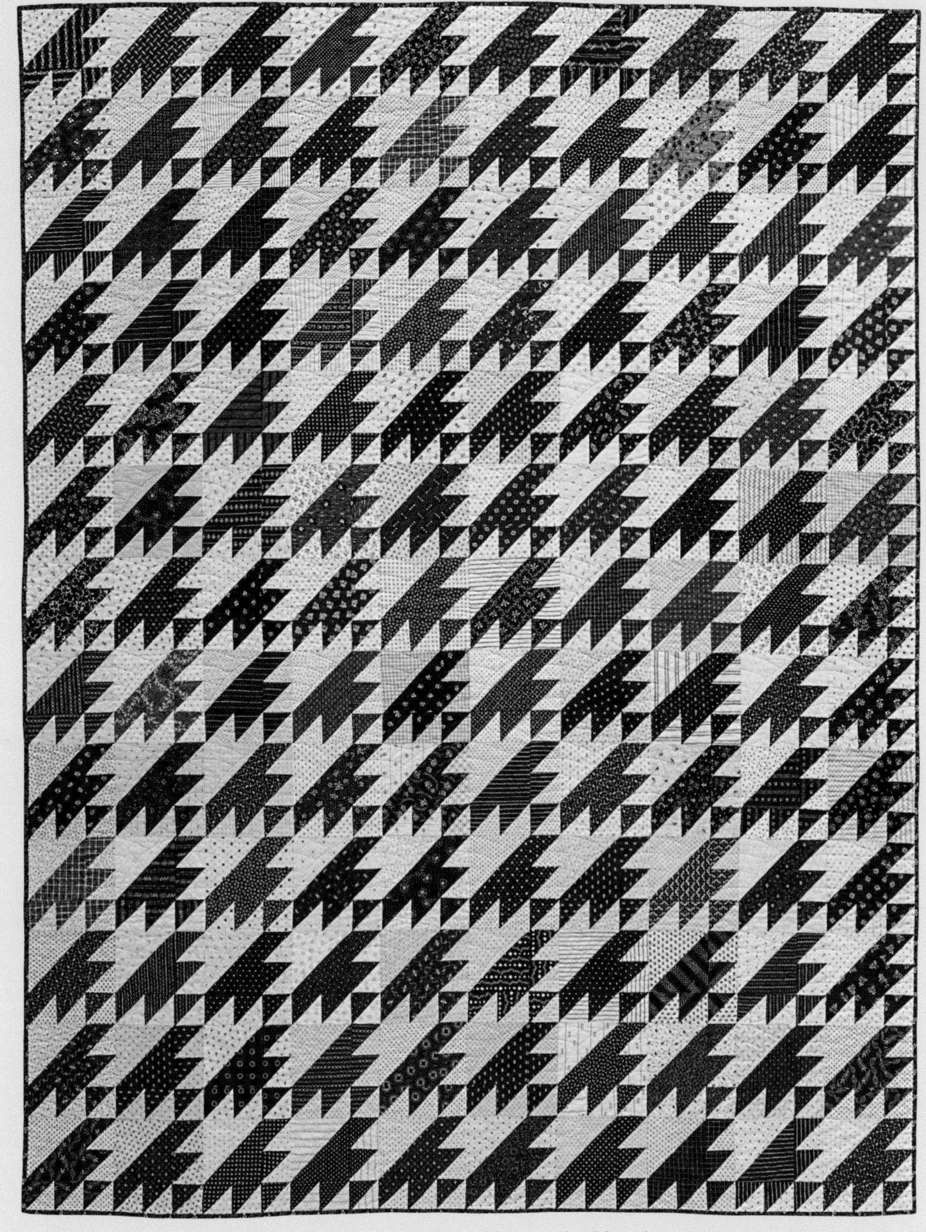

Designed and made by Annette Plog, quilted by Sheri Mecom

Westward Ships

Finished quilt: 60″ × 78″ • **Finished block:** 6″ × 6″

The Lost Ship block was often seen during the 1800s. The popularity of indigo-and-white (or indigo-and-light) quilts continued, and they still endure as a favorite of many. Remember to use different shades of lights, from white to cream, for the sparkle. I also used some grays and mourning prints in this quilt for variety.

This quilt was the product of a block exchange with friends. Block exchanges are invaluable when your goal is scrappy. Maybe this quilt could be your stitch group's next project!

Materials

Refer to What Size to Buy for a Scrappy Look? (at right) to see how many blocks you can cut from various cuts of fabric.

Lights: 4½ yards total of assorted light and cream shirtings

Darks: 4½ yards total of assorted navy blues, blacks, grays, and indigos

Binding: ½ yard

Backing: 5 yards

Batting: 68″ × 86″

Cutting

Lost Ship blocks

Lost Ship block

Follow these instructions to cut enough pieces for 2 Lost Ship blocks. Keep the pieces together. You will need to cut enough pieces for 130 blocks.

From the lights:

- Cut 1 square 5″ × 5″.
- Cut 5 squares 3″ × 3″.

From the darks:

- Cut 1 square 5″ × 5″.
- Cut 5 squares 3″ × 3″.

Tip

What Size to Buy for a Scrappy Look?

There are 130 blocks in this quilt. The blocks are made from 2 sizes of half-square triangles, and you can cut squares for 2 blocks at a time. Here are some guidelines about how many blocks you can cut from various yardages. See Cutting (pages 65 and 66) for cutting diagrams.

- **Layer cakes (10″ squares):** 2 blocks from each pair of squares, with a bit of waste. Buy 65 light and 65 dark squares.
- **Fat quarters:** 6 blocks from each pair of fat quarters, or 8 blocks if you cut carefully and your fat quarter has at least 17″ × 20″ of usable space. Some fat quarters may have only 16″ × 20″ of usable space if the rectangle is crooked, prewashed, or miscut. In those cases, you could piece together the last 2 smaller squares to make enough for 8 blocks. For 8 blocks from a pair of fat quarters, you'll need 17 darks and 17 lights.
- **Standard ¼ yard:** 8 blocks from each pair, if you cut carefully and have at least 8″ of usable space all the way across the yardage. Otherwise, 6 blocks with a little waste. For 8 blocks from a ¼-yard cut, you'll need 17 darks and 17 lights.
- **Fat eighths:** 4 blocks from each pair. For 4 blocks from a pair of fat eighths, you'll need 33 darks and 33 lights.

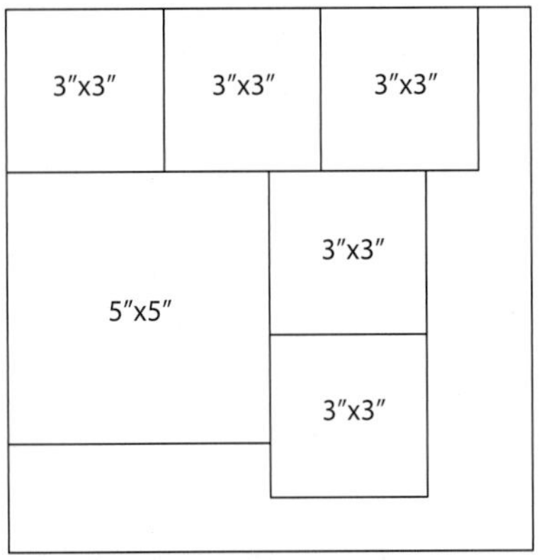

Cutting diagram for a 10″ square

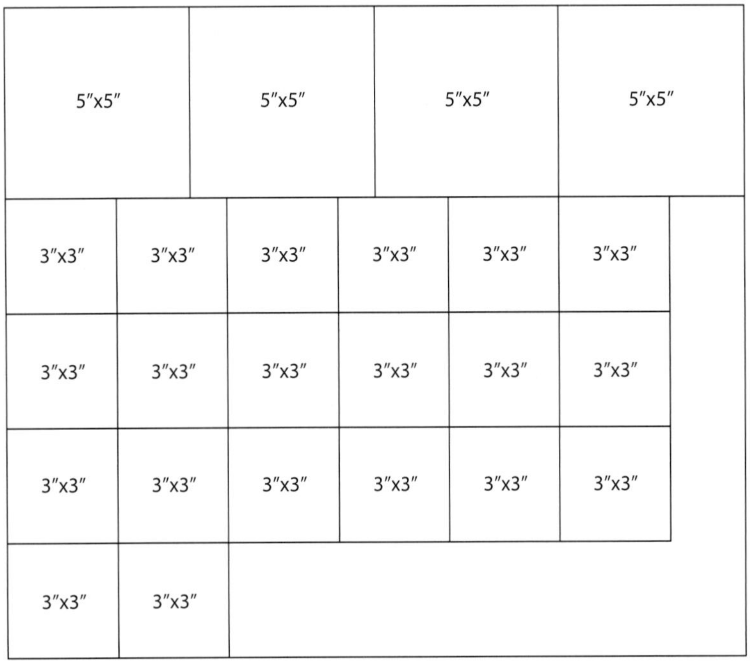

Cutting diagram for a fat quarter. If the fat quarter is not long enough to cut the last 2 small squares, piece them from the leftover fabric.

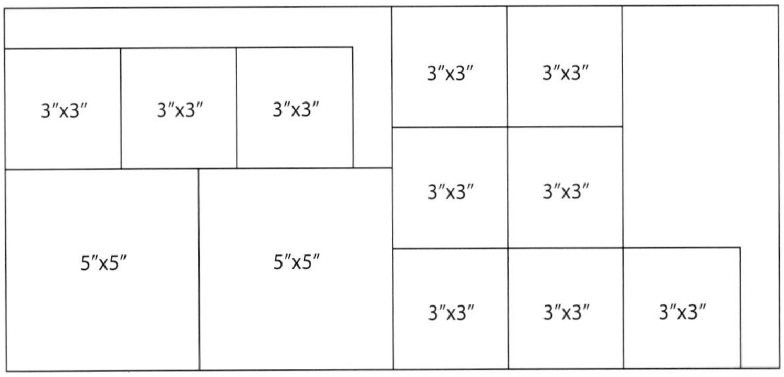

Cutting diagram for a fat eighth

Construction

Lost Ship Block

Use matching fabrics to make each block.

1. Refer to Making Half-Square Triangles (page 12) for sewing instructions. Pair a light and a dark 5″ × 5″ square to make 2 half-square triangles 4½″ × 4½″.

2. Pair 5 light and 5 dark 3″ × 3″ squares to make 10 half-square triangles measuring 2½″ × 2½″.

3. Referring to the block assembly diagram, arrange 5 small half-square triangles and 1 larger half-square triangle.

4. Sew together 2 half-square triangles in a vertical row. Press the seam allowance toward the bottom of the row.

5. Sew the vertical row to the right side of the larger half-square triangle. Press the seam allowance toward the large piece.

6. Sew together 3 half-square triangles in a horizontal row. Press the seam allowances toward the right.

Block assembly

7. Sew the row from Step 6 to the larger half-square triangle unit. Either press the seam up, or use the clip trick shown in Sewing Basics (page 14).

Lost Ship block

8. Repeat Steps 1–7 to make 130 Lost Ship blocks.

Quilt Assembly

1. Referring to the quilt assembly diagram (at right), arrange 13 rows of 10 blocks each, with the colors distributed in a pleasing manner.

2. Sew the blocks in each row together, and then sew the rows together to complete the top.

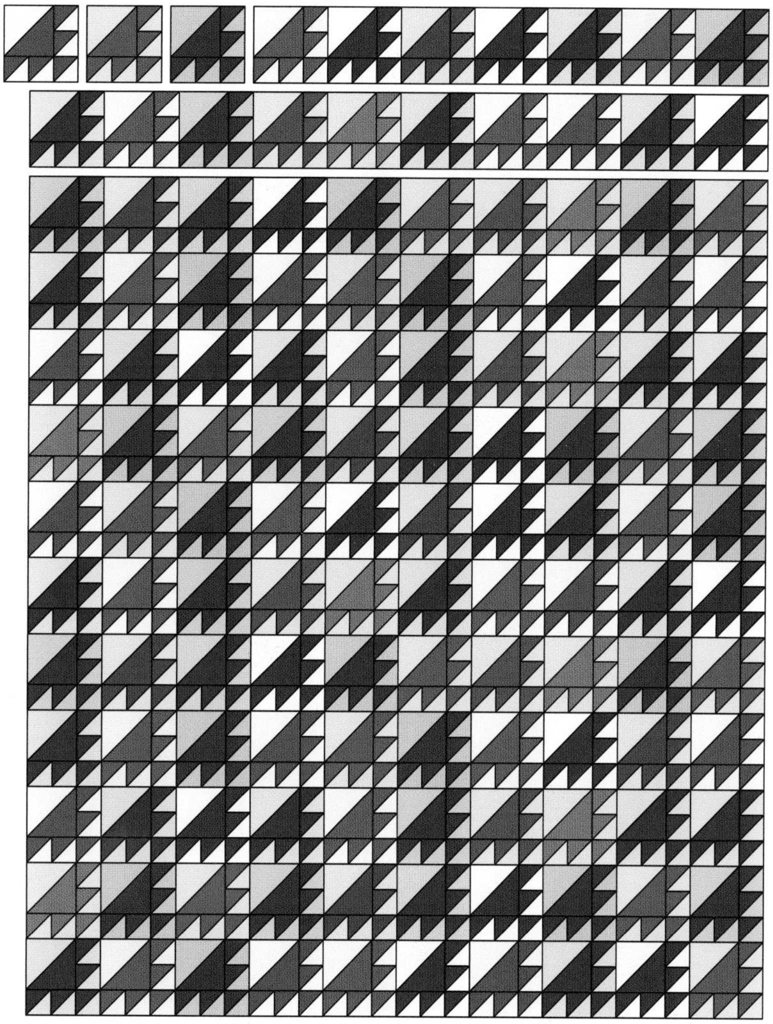

Quilt assembly

Finishing

Quilt using a favorite quilt design. This one is machine quilted using an overall fan design. Follow Finishing Your Quilt (page 14) to bind your quilt, and enjoy.

Designed and made by Annette Plog, quilted by Sheri Mecom

Bows and Ties

Finished quilt: 62½″ × 85″ • **Finished block:** 5″ × 5″

In the late 1800s the Bow Tie quilt was a standard, as seen in many of the antiques left from that time. I used woven plaids and stripes, greens, cadet blues, and indigos for making the bow ties. This project would make a great masculine quilt with the darker prints and plaids. The fabrics remind me of my grandfather's shirts and ties.

Materials

Light: 1⅜ yards for the blocks, plus 2½ yards for the sashing

Darks: ¼ yard each of 8 different blacks, greens, indigos, tans, and cadet blues

Cornerstones: 1 yard of indigo

Binding: ½ yard

Backing: 5¼ yards

Batting: 70″ × 93″

Cutting

Bow Tie blocks

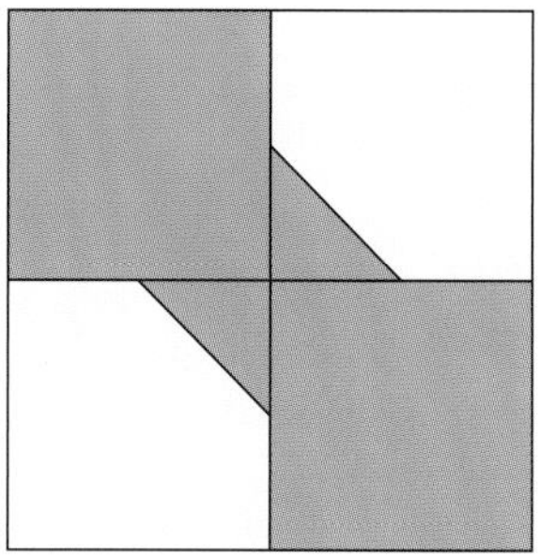

Bow Tie block

You will be able to cut enough dark pieces from each ¼ yard to yield 12 blocks. You will need 88 blocks.

From the light:

- Cut 192 squares 3″ × 3″.

From *each* dark:

- Cut 24 squares 3″ × 3″.
- Cut 24 squares 1¾″ × 1¾″.

Sashing

- Cut 28 strips 3″ × width of fabric.

  Subcut 195 rectangles 3″ × 5½″.

Cornerstones

- Cut 9 strips 3″ × width of fabric.

  Subcut 108 squares 3″ × 3″.

Construction

Bow Tie Block

Use matching fabrics for each block.

1. Right sides together, place a dark 1¾″ × 1¾″ square on the right top corner of a light 3″ × 3″ square. On the back of the dark square, draw a diagonal line from corner to corner. Sew on the line.

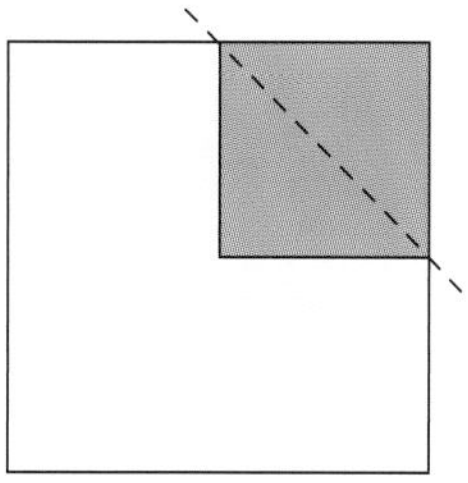

2. Cut away the seam allowance ¼″ from the sewn line. Press the seam allowance toward the dark fabric.

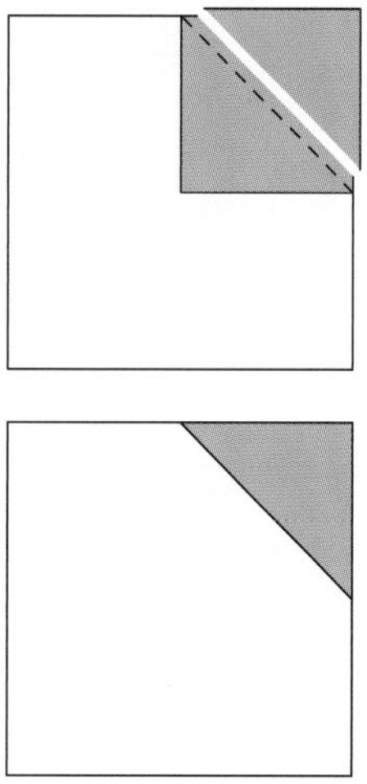

3. Repeat Steps 1 and 2 to make a matching triangle/square unit.

4. Arrange the 2 triangle/square units and 2 matching 3″ × 3″ squares in 2 rows. Sew the units in the top row together and then the units in the bottom row together.

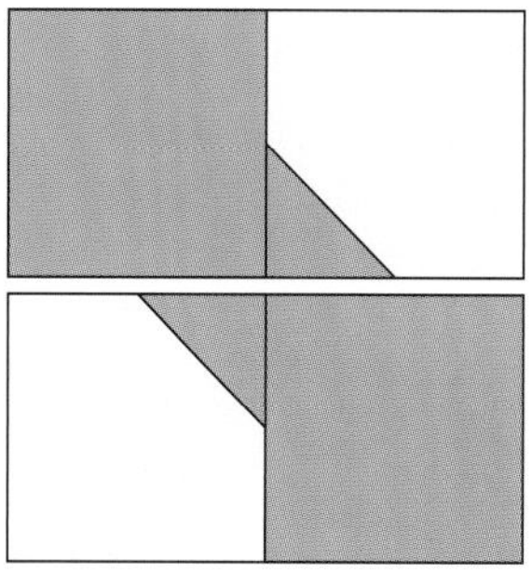

5. Sew the block halves together to complete a block measuring 5½″ × 5½″. Make 11 more blocks from the same color combination.

6. Using the remaining dark and light fabrics, repeat Steps 1–5 to create a total of 96 Bow Tie blocks. You will only need 88 blocks for the quilt. The extra blocks will give you flexibility in block placement.

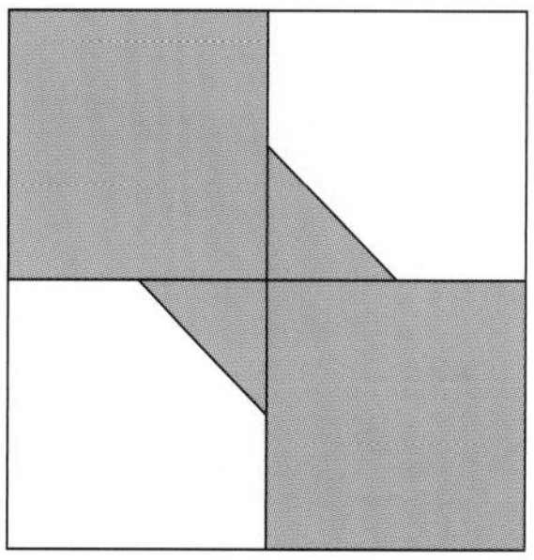

Bow Tie block. Make 12 blocks in each color combination, 96 total.

Sashing Strips

Arrange 9 cornerstone squares and 8 sashing rectangles in a row, beginning and ending the row with the cornerstones. Sew the units together, pressing seam allowances toward the sashing rectangles. Make 12 sashing strips.

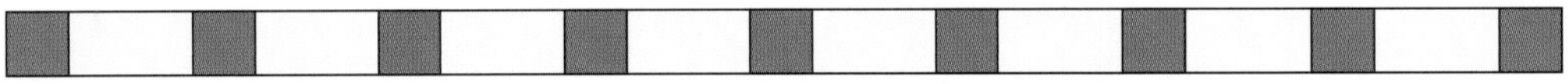

Sashing strip. Make 12.

Quilt Assembly

1. Referring to the quilt assembly diagram (at right), lay out the Bow Tie blocks in 11 rows of 8 blocks each, taking care to place the various fabrics in a pleasing manner. Place a sashing rectangle between each block and at both ends of each row.

2. Sew the blocks and sashing rectangles in each row together. Press the seam allowance toward the sashing rectangles.

3. Place the sashing strips between each row and at the top and bottom of the quilt. Starting at the top of the quilt, sew the rows together to complete the top.

Finishing

Quilt using a favorite quilt design. This one is machine quilted using an overall fan design. Follow Finishing Your Quilt (page 14) to bind your quilt, and enjoy.

Quilt assembly

Designed, made, and quilted by Annette Plog

Homespun Plaid Table Topper

Finished table topper: 28″ × 28″ • **Finished block:** 3½″ × 3½″

Homespun or woven fabrics always give a warm, cozy feeling. This table topper is scrappy and easy to make. It is a wonderful beginner project. Have fun mixing all the different fabrics. Mix in some "ugly" fabrics and see how they can really shine!

Materials

1 pack of precut squares 10″ × 10″: at least 16 pieces (8 light and 8 medium/dark) *or* the following:

Lights: 8 fat quarters *or* ¼ yard each of 8 light homespuns

Mediums and darks: 8 fat quarters *or* ¼ yard each of 8 blue and gray homespuns

Binding: ⅓ yard

Backing: 1 yard

Batting: 32″ × 32″

> ### Tip
>
> **Using Precuts**
>
> For this little quilt I used a layer cake pack: a group of coordinating precut squares 10″ × 10″. Since the fabrics were from a single line, they all coordinated perfectly.
>
> As a rule I do not like to limit myself to fabrics from only one line. I like to pull from my stash, using many different lines, to give a more interesting look. But sometimes a project lends itself to using precuts. It can be a simpler, less expensive way of acquiring many different fabrics cut in the size you need—just right for your project.
>
> Many fabric manufacturers offer precuts in different sizes, from the smallest of squares to fat-quarter bundles. Go ahead and give them a try. I really like the simplicity of choosing fabrics, the price, and the number of different fabrics. I think you will, too!

Cutting

Hourglass blocks

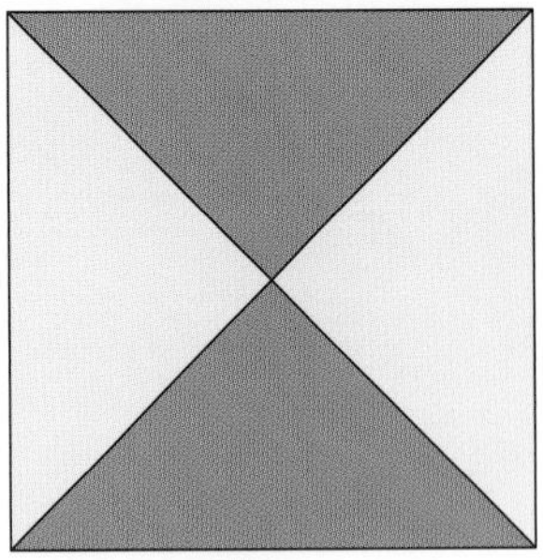

Hourglass block

Precut squares

From *each* light 10″ × 10″ square:

- Cut 4 squares 5″ × 5″, for a total of 32 squares.

From *each* dark 10″ × 10″ square:

- Cut 4 squares 5″ × 5″, for a total of 32 squares.

or

Fat quarters

From *each* light fat-quarter or ¼ yard:

- Cut 4 squares 5″ × 5″, for a total of 32 squares.

From *each* dark fat-quarter or ¼ yard:

- Cut 4 squares 5″ × 5″, for a total of 32 squares.

Construction

Hourglass Block

1. Refer to Making Hourglass Blocks (page 13) for sewing instructions. Use the 5″ × 5″ light and dark squares to make 64 blocks that measure 3½″ × 3½″.

Hourglass block. Make 64.

> *Tip*
>
> **Working with Homespun Fabrics**
>
> Homespun fabrics are not as tightly woven as printed fabrics. They tend to stretch when you are working with them. Here is a quick tip for handling homespun fabrics: Spray the fabric lightly with a spray starch or spray sizing. After you have cut your 5″ × 5″ squares, lightly spray and press the fabric. Your fabric will have more body and will not stretch as much, keeping your block closer to the desired size.

Quilt Assembly

1. Referring to the quilt assembly diagram (below), arrange the blocks in 8 rows of 8 blocks each. Place the various fabrics in a pleasing manner.

2. Sew the blocks in each row together. Then sew the rows together to complete the quilt top.

Quilt assembly

Finishing

Quilt using a favorite quilt design. This one is machine quilted using an overall grid design. Follow Finishing Your Quilt (page 14) to bind your quilt, and enjoy.

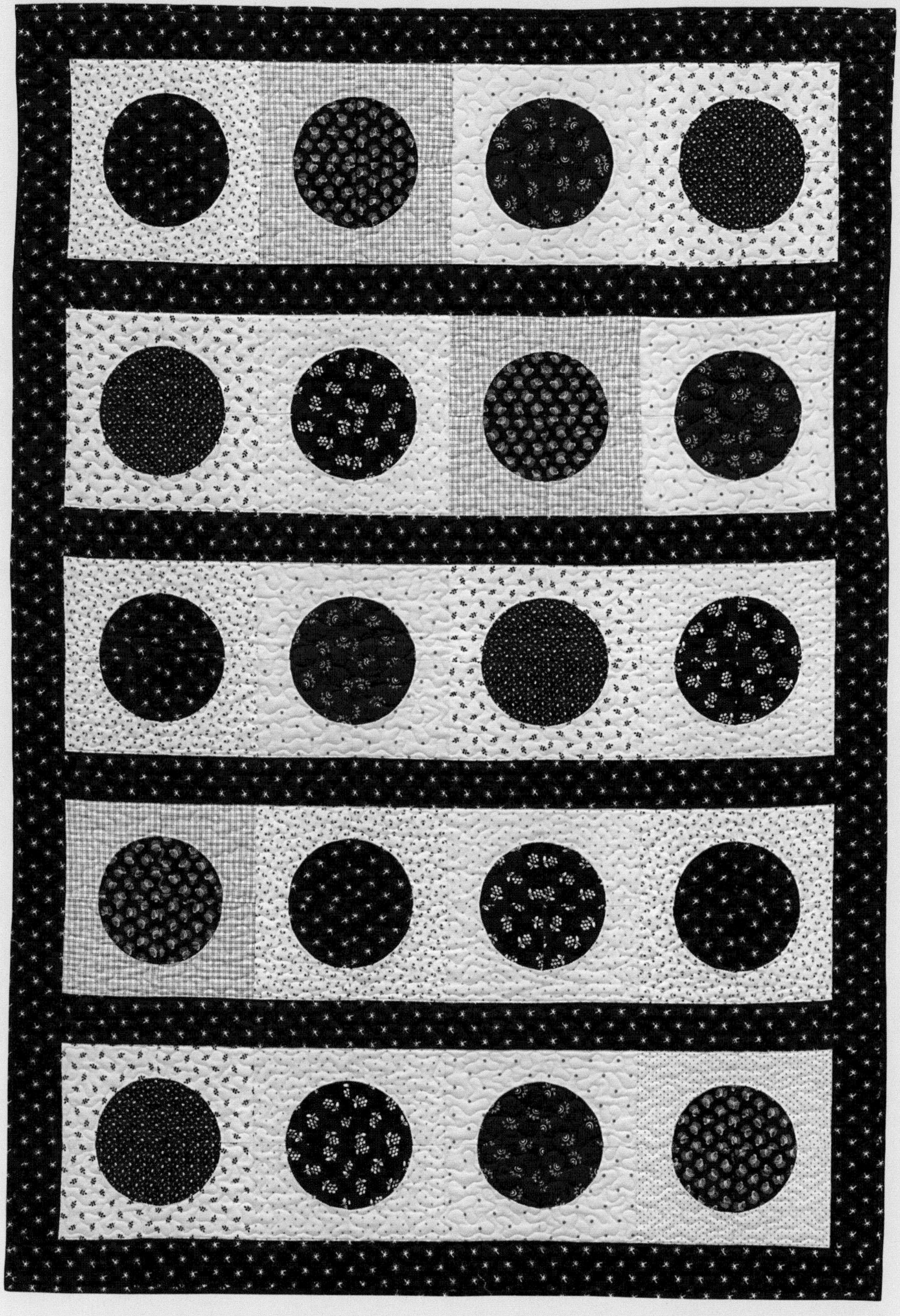

Designed and made by Annette Plog, quilted by Kerry Coburn

Dot, Dot, Dash

Finished quilt: 36″ × 52″ • **Finished block:** 8″ × 8″

Dot, Dot, Dash uses curved piecing. Don't be intimidated; it is not hard. The cute Polka Dot block makes this quilt bold, striking, and fun. The contrasting indigo and light shirting are just perfect for a child's quilt with a modern vibe.

Materials

Lights: 3/8 yard each of 5 shirtings

Darks: 3/8 yard each of 5 indigos

Sashing and border: 1½ yards of indigo

Binding: 3/8 yard

Backing: 2½ yards

Batting: 44″ × 60″

Cutting

Polka Dot blocks

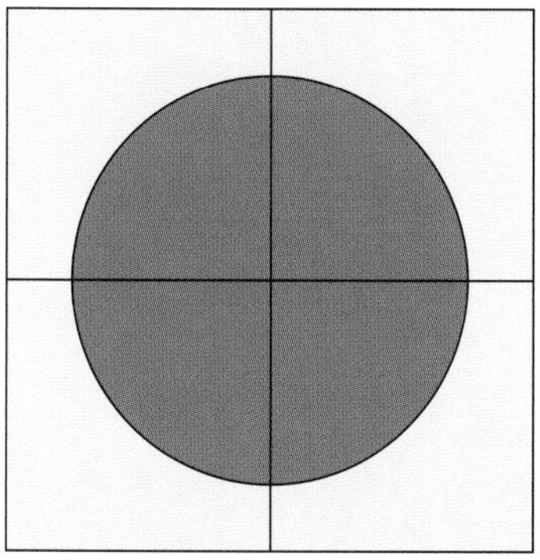

Polka Dot block

From template plastic or your favorite template material, create a template using patterns A and B (page 78).

From *each* light:

- Cut 16 of piece A.

From *each* indigo:

- Cut 16 of piece B.

Sashing

- On the *length* of the fabric, cut 4 strips 2½″ × 32½″.

Border

You may want to cut your strips a little longer in case your quilt turns out to be a slightly different size than the pattern size. You may trim them after you have assembled the quilt top.

On the *length* of the fabric:

- Cut 2 strips 2½″ × 48½″ for the side borders.
- Cut 2 strips 2½″ × 36½″ for the top and bottom borders.

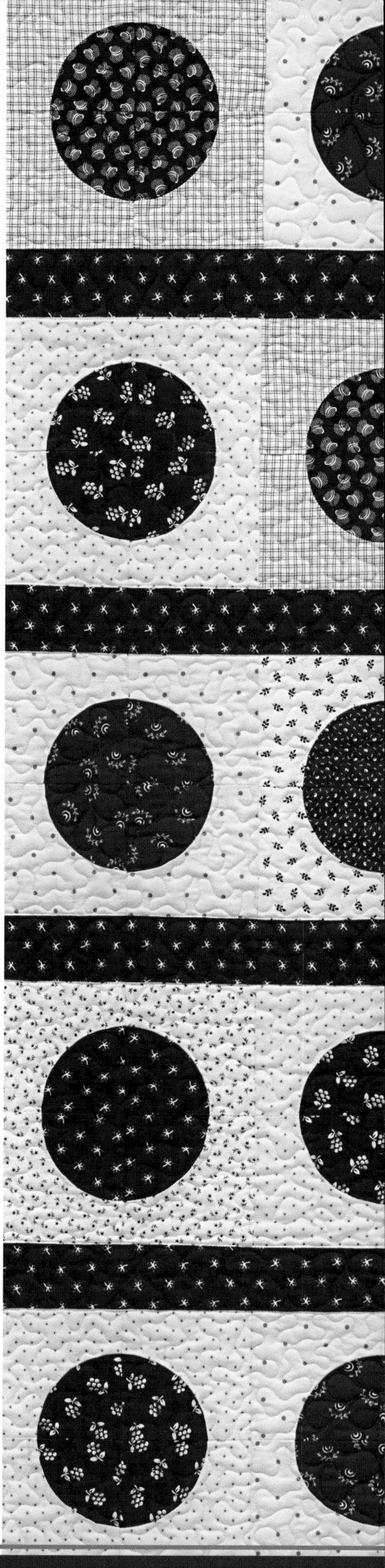

Construction

Polka Dot Block

1. Choose a piece A and a piece B, and mark the center of the curve in each. Right sides together, pin the blocks together at the center points.

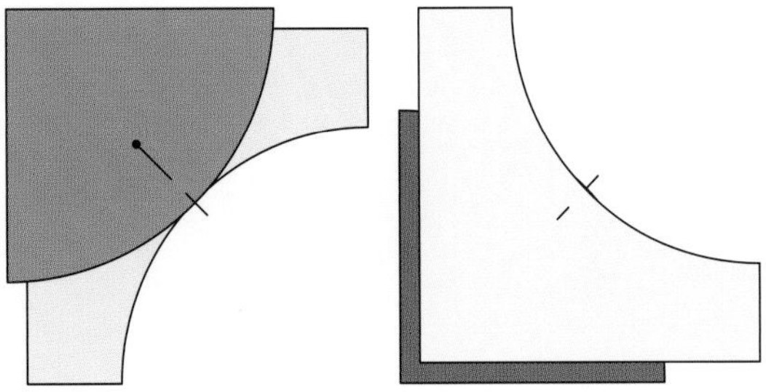

2. Pin 1 corner and ease the curve together, pinning along the curve.

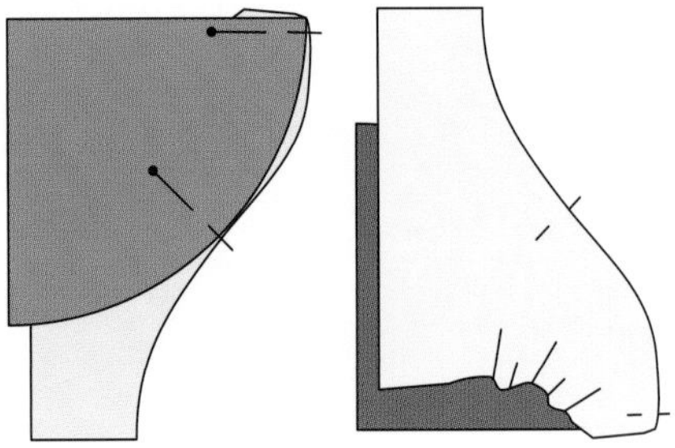

3. Pin the opposite corner and ease the curve together, pinning along the curve.

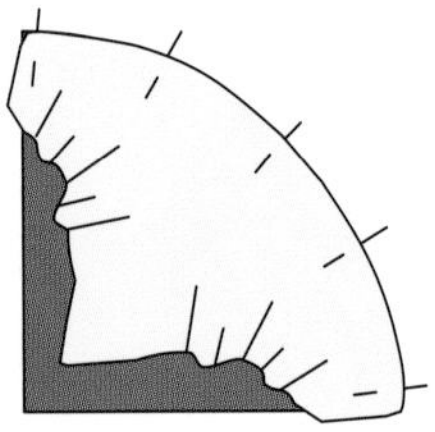

4. Sew the curved seam together, easing as you curve. This seam is cut on the bias, so it stretches and eases in. Press the curved seam toward the dark fabric.

5. Repeat Steps 1–4 to make 3 more blocks from the same fabrics. On 2 blocks, press the seam allowance toward the dark fabric. On the other 2 blocks, press the seam allowance toward the light. No clipping is necessary because the seams are on the bias and will stretch into place easily.

6. Arrange the blocks in 2 halves, dark quarter-circles together, and matching the opposite pressed seams. Sew the top pair together and then the bottom pair together.

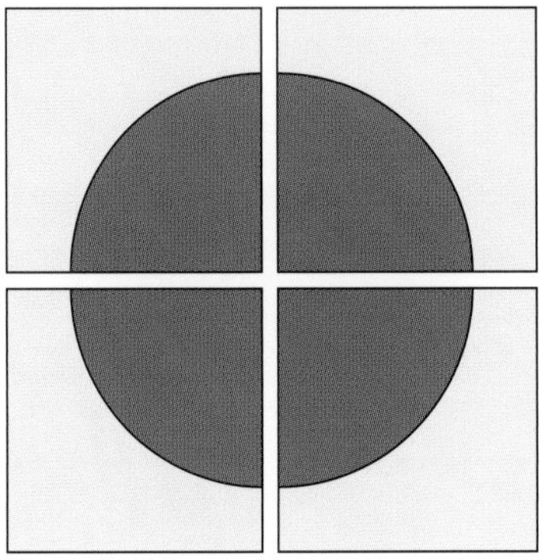

7. Sew the 2 sets together to form a block measuring 8½″ × 8½″.

8. Repeat Steps 1–7 to make a total of 20 large blocks.

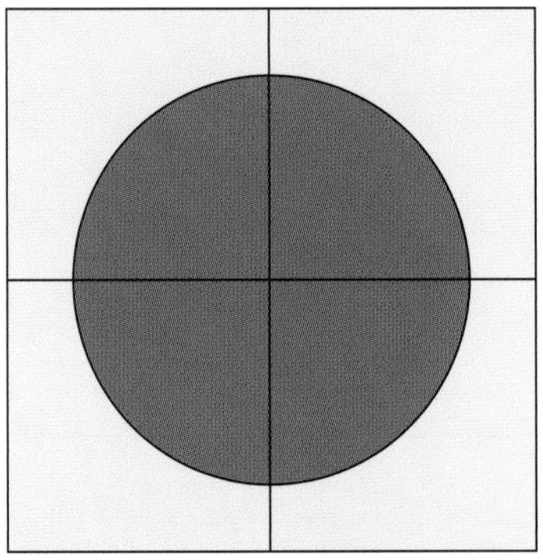

Polka Dot block. Make 20.

Quilt Assembly

1. Referring to the quilt assembly diagram (at right), arrange the blocks in 5 rows of 4 blocks each, taking care to place the various fabrics in a pleasing manner.

2. Sew the blocks in each row together.

3. Sew the rows together with a 2½" × 32½" sashing strip between the rows. Press the seam allowances toward the sashing.

4. Sew a 2½" × 48½" border strip to each side of the quilt top. Press the seam allowances toward the border. Sew a 2½" × 36½" border strip to the top and bottom of the quilt to complete the top. Press the seam allowances toward the border.

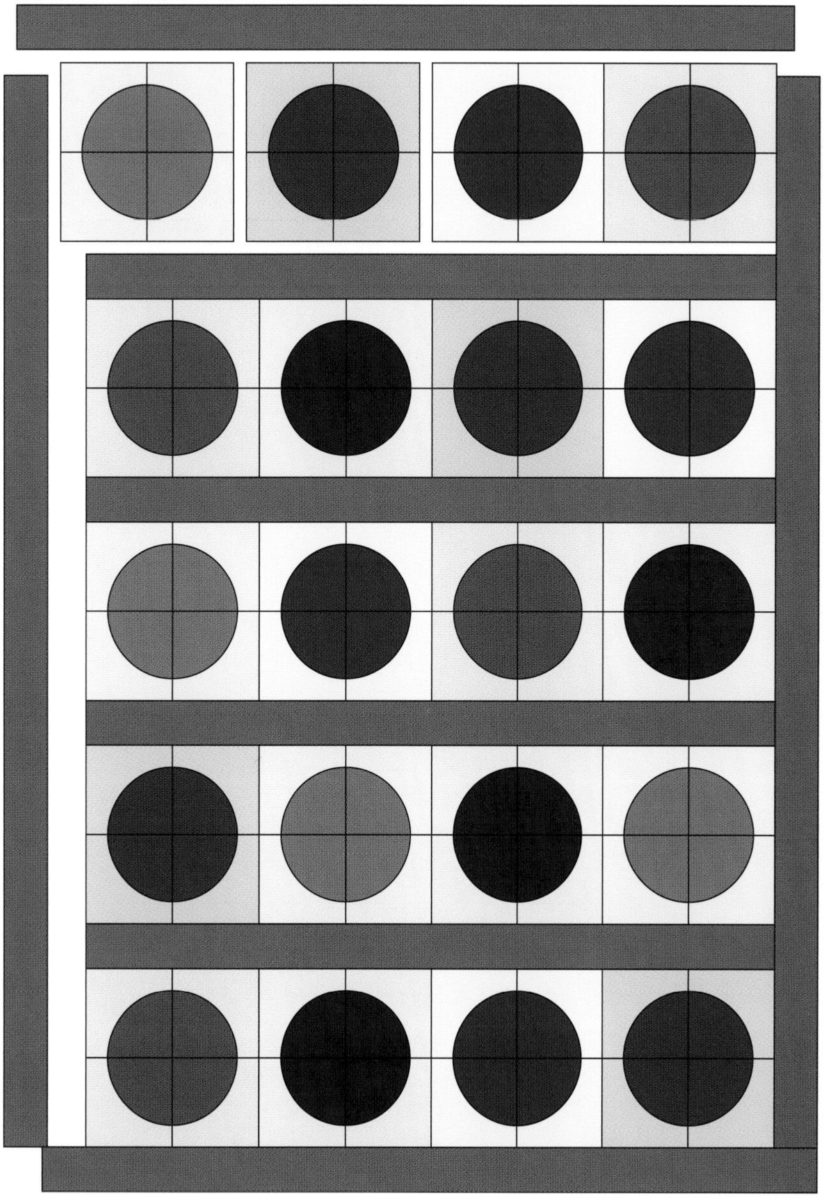

Quilt assembly

Finishing

Quilt using a favorite quilt design. This one is machine quilted using an overall grid design. Follow Finishing Your Quilt (page 14) to bind your quilt, and enjoy.

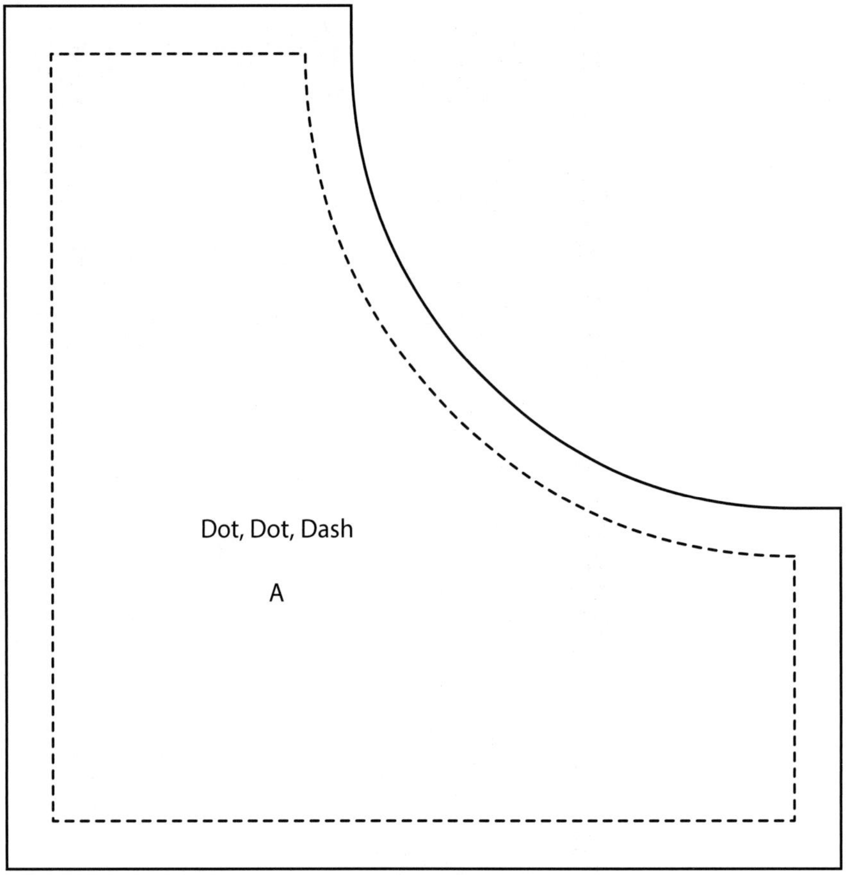

Polka Dot block, A

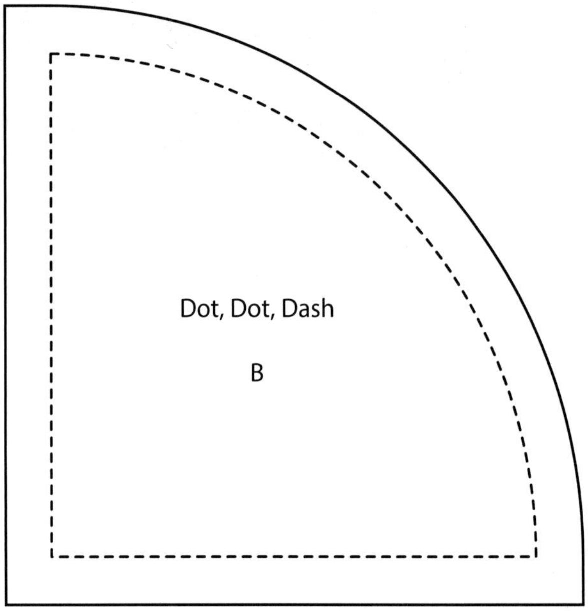

Polka Dot block, B

About the Author

Photo by Annette Plog Photography

Annette learned to sew, embroider, paint, and garden from her grandmother. She learned to quilt with the goal of making quilts that would someday be family heirlooms. Her mom, Jacque, instilled in Annette a love and appreciation for antiques. Because most of her family's quilts and heirlooms had been stolen or destroyed, there were no antique quilts for passing down. It seemed the perfect void to fill.

In 1997 a talented group of ladies asked Annette to join their block-exchange group with the purpose of reproducing antique quilts. The group, known as the Nineteenth-Century Patchwork Divas, would choose a quilt and have a block exchange, and a wonderful scrappy reproduction quilt would be the result. Because choosing the reproduction fabrics specific to the time was important, knowledge of antique fabrics was necessary. Annette learned more about antique fabrics through classes, friends, research, and antique dealers. She has learned so much since she has been involved with the Divas, but the learning never ends. With each block exchange, there is more to learn—whether it is finding the perfect reproduction blue for an 1870s quilt or perfecting a Y-seam.

Annette loves sewing, photography, gardening, running, antiquing at Round Top, and watching the grandkids.

She and her husband of 40 years, Jim, live in Dalworthington Gardens, Texas. They have 2 children, Lauren and David; 3 grandchildren, Lucy, Joshua, and Riley; and a border collie mix named Jake.

Resources

Books on Dating Fabrics

America's Printed Fabrics 1770–1890, by Barbara Brackman (C&T Publishing)

A Time Traveler's Guide to Printed Cottons, Volume 1, by Margo Krager

Dating Fabrics—A Color Guide: 1800–1960, by Eileen Jahnke Trestain (American Quilter's Society)

Fabric Manufacturers Offering Reproduction Fabric Lines

Moda Fabrics • *modafabrics.com*

Andover Fabrics • *andoverfabrics.com*

Windham Fabrics • *windhamfabrics.com*

Marcus Fabrics • *marcusfabrics.com*

Want even more creative content?
Go to ctpub.com/offer
& sign up to receive our gift to you!
MENU
C&T PUBLISHING
Your Home for Creative Quilting & Sewing
HAND PRINTING STUDIO
Print on Almost Anything!
Get some in-spiration
GET INSPIRED
GARMENT SEWING LOOKBOOK 2016
Make it, snap it, share it
using #ctpublishing